Rachel's Children

CONTEMPORARY NATIVE AMERICAN COMMUNITIES
Stepping Stones to the Seventh Generation

Acknowledging the strength and vibrancy of Native American people and nations today, this series examines life in contemporary Native American communities from the point of view of Native concerns and values. These new publications are intended to be correctives to the misconceptions that still appear in many books and in the American imagination: that Indian people largely disappeared or were assimilated after 1890. Books in the series cover topics that are of cultural and political importance to tribal peoples and that affect their possibilities for survival, in both urban and rural communities.

SERIES EDITORS:
Troy Johnson
American Indian Studies
California State University, Long Beach
Long Beach, CA 90840
trj@csulb.edu

Duane Champagne
Native Nations Law and Policy Center
292 Haines Hall
Box 951551
University of California, Los Angeles
Los Angeles, CA 90095-1551
champagn@ucla.edu

BOOKS IN THE SERIES
1. *Inuit, Whaling, and Sustainability*, Milton M. R. Freeman, Ingmar Egede, Lyudmila Bogoslovskaya, Igor G. Krupnik, Richard A. Caulfield and Marc G. Stevenson (1999)
2. *Contemporary Native American Political Issues*, edited by Troy Johnson (1999)
3. *Contemporary Native American Cultural Issues*, edited by Duane Champagne (1999)
4. *Modern Tribal Development: Paths to Self Sufficiency and Cultural Integrity in Indian Country*, Dean Howard Smith (2000)
5. *American Indians and the Urban Experience*, edited by Susan Lobo and Kurt Peters (2000)
6. *Medicine Ways: Disease, Health, and Survival among Native Americans*, edited by Clifford Trafzer and Diane Weiner (2000)
7. *Native American Studies in Higher Education: Models for Collaboration between Universities and Indigenous Nations*, edited by Duane Champagne and Jay Stauss (2002)
8. *Spider Woman Walks This Land: Traditional Cultural Properties and the Navajo Nation*, by Kelli Carmean (2002)
9. *Alaska Native Political Leadership and Higher Education: One University, Two Universes*, by Michael Jennings (2004)
10. *Indigenous Intellectual Property Rights: Legal Obstacles and Innovative Solutions*, edited by Mary Riley (2004)
11. *Healing and Mental Health for Native Americans: Speaking in Red*, edited by Ethan Nebelkopf and Mary Phillips (2004)
12. *Rachel's Children*, by Lois Beardslee (2004)

Rachel's Children

Stories from a Contemporary Native American Woman

Lois Beardslee

A Division of
ROWMAN & LITTLEFIELD PUBLISHERS, INC.
Lanham • Boulder • New York • Toronto • Plymouth, UK

ALTAMIRA PRESS
A division of Rowman & Littlefield Publishers, Inc.
4501 Forbes Boulevard, Suite 200
Lanham, MD 20706

Estover Road
Plymouth PL6 7PY
United Kingdon

British Library Cataloguing in Publication Information Available

Library of Congress Cataloging-in-Publication Data

Beardslee, Lois.
  Rachel's children : stories from a contemporary Native American woman / Lois
Beardslee.
    p. cm. — (Contemporary Native American communities ; v. 12)
  Includes bibliographical references.
  ISBN 0-7591-0689-4 (hardcover : alk. paper) — ISBN 0-7591-0690-8 (pbk. : alk.
paper)
  1. Indians of North America—Fiction. 2. Indian women—Fiction. I. Title.
II. Series.

  PS3602.E255R33 2004
  813'.6—dc22

                                                              2004001026

Printed in the United States of America

⊗™ The paper used in this publication meets the minimum requirements of American
National Standard for Information Sciences—Permanence of Paper for Printed Library
Materials, ANSI/NISO Z39.48-1992.

For my children

CONTENTS

CONTENTS

CHAPTER ONE

ON A CLEAR DAY
INDIANS CAN SEE FOREVER

"I didn't know Manaboozhou had a wife."

"Oh yeah, he had children, siblings, cousins, aunts, uncles, friends, neighbors. . . . As a matter of fact, I just got a letter from a man whose father's mother was the sister of my grandmother's brother's wife. Apparently the two girls were from the Hazelnut family. The Hazelnut family . . . Remind me later to talk about the Hazelnut family.

"So the one sister, she died very young, very early on in the marriage. They didn't have any children. Uncle Lenny, he didn't know it then, because he was such a young man, but he'd always wanted children. No doubt about that. You know the hours he always spent with us? Involuntary. The man never wanted to be alone.

"She drowned. She was only nineteen."

"How did she drown?"

"No. No, no. . . . I don't want to talk about that. Too many drownings, you know. Horrible. It's a horrible way to die. No more. I don't want to talk about it."

"What's the significance of the sisters?"

"Well, they were related to us by marriage, you see. He never remarried, Great Uncle Leonard. He stayed a part of them, that other family. He fished for the old man, because all he had was girls. He needed sons-in-law, and Josephine was already married."

"Who was Josephine?"

"The sister. The older sister of Lennie's dead wife. She was married to an Asawmik."

"And?"

"Grandson."

"Grandson?"

"Grandson. My cousin, Zane. He's seventy-eight."

"Your cousin is seventy-eight?"

"Well, he's not my first cousin. And it was a big family with a lot of kids. Those kids spanned generations. My uncle we called the Little Dragonfly, he was only two years older than my oldest sister. He was my mom's littlest brother. . . . He drowned, too. Playing. Just playing out there in the boat. Just poor judgment, that's all.

"My mom got mad and said it was our fault, because we were always bothering him. The boat was the only place he could be alone. Some really soggy comic books washed up all that next week after he died.

"But it wasn't us that made him show off and do dumb things. He was always standing up in that boat, and it was too little for a stand-up boat. . . . We didn't make him that way. It was growing up without his parents, having to have his big sister take care of him. She got busy with her own family, and there was no one there to cuddle him any more. . . . So you see, we didn't drown him."

"Of course you didn't."

"Used to think so, though. Couldn't read a comic book for years." Rachel looks down, ashamed of herself, for no good reason.

"So the generations aren't really that far apart. Do you understand?" She asks as though my understanding will buy her forgiveness for some unknown sins.

I nod. I am not sure, but I think I understand. I only have one sister. We are two years apart. But my parents and their siblings came from larger families. Their births spanned decades. That generation, by virtue of its breadth, is a link to more than one generation past.

"So your seventy-eight-year-old not-first-cousin is related to your great uncle by marriage?"

"Yeah, but see, it's those Hazelnut girls. *They* were his family."

"Whose family?"

"Manaboozhou's family. There. You see? His wife was a Hazelnut."

"Was she really a hazelnut, or was she a person?"

"Hazelnut. That was her family name. We don't turn nuts into people. People turn into nuts sometimes, but that's different."

I am laughing. "OK, so Manaboozhou's wife's maiden name was Hazelnut."

"Maiden name is about as close as you could call it. But we don't really reckon our relations quite that way."

"But she was a Hazelnut?"

"Yup."

"And?"

"Now, you know right away what latitude that family came from, 'cause those hazelnuts only grow in that one band that runs east-west along the northern shores of the big lakes, and along the southern shore of the biggest. We talk about these, the world's largest cluster of freshwater seas, as though they are mere beaver ponds. . . . Do you see? Do you see how big our family is? Do you see how big our history is?"

"Yes, I am beginning to see it. It surprises me, but I'm beginning to see it. Does every family have a spirit that it is descended from?"

"Minwaudeniimikwe wasn't a spirit."

"Who was Minwaudeniimikwe?"

"Minwaudeniimikwe was Manaboozhou's wife."

"She wasn't a spirit?"

"Of course not. She was just one of those Hazelnut girls."

"I thought she would be a spirit," I say.

"No. No way. Could you imagine two spirits married to each other? They'd be in trouble all the time. No, one of them has to be human. One of them has to be the voice of reason.

"Manaboozhou was always getting in trouble. He was half spirit and half human, you know. His father was the West Wind. Wasn't around much to raise the boys. Wiinona, his mother, she died right after she had him. Manaboozhou's grandmother raised him. Did a pretty good job, too. He was half human, you know—tough kid to raise."

"I would imagine."

"He spent most of his life along those shores, where the hazelnuts grew. They were the nicest places on the lakes. The Anishnabeg, the first people, we call ourselves, they planted them all over the place."

"Hazelnuts were not wild?"

"Oh yes, heavens, yes, they are wild. But they are domesticated, too. One can travel for weeks with a dormant spring stick, using it for bracing on a pack, then, later, in a new location, put it in water to root. Then it should be planted someplace where it will get moisture, but won't be washed away by high water. The bottomlands near the big lakes are best. They get plenty of moisture that way, but they don't bloom until the big lakes warm up, so the blooms don't freeze out."

"I don't think I've ever seen a hazelnut bloom. I don't think I've ever seen a hazelnut," I confess.

"Not very impressive. Just a bush, really. And the blooms are rusty-green dangly things. You wouldn't even know they were blooming, not like a rose. But they are the first things to bloom come spring, so we always keep an eye out for them. They seem to like it a bit cool, so they stay around the upper fringes of the big lakes, except for the biggest lake. There they just grow around the southern fringes. I told you, they grow in a band, not too far south, not too far north. And they are always at the nicest, most hospitable spots on the lakes."

"Why?"

"Because that's where *we* lived!"

I am amazed how often she speaks of them as *we*, these generations long past, these offspring of supernaturals. I am amazed, because, as she pointed out, she does talk of these Great Lakes as mere tameable bodies of water. Lake Superior she merely refers to as "the biggest." It is the largest freshwater lake in the world. Its shores gave up more mineral wealth than the great California Gold Rush.

It has become impossible for me to distinguish the tall, dark woman from her landscape. I cannot imagine her thriving outside of this setting. Yet she has told me stories about being away, to college, to the desert, to cities. I have seen her weep and wring her hands and long to return to her remote bush camps. I cannot imagine her in a grocery store. Only last week, she mailed me some wild cranberry muffins.

"Delicious. Share your recipe," I said into the receiver.

"Jiffy Mix," she had answered.

"I'm so surprised. I'd think you, of all people, would make them from scratch."

"On a good day, it takes twenty minutes to climb the cliff to get up to where the cranberries grow. Imagine doing it in subfreezing weather, with a four-year-old. Jesus, and you want me to make the muffins from scratch?"

4

CHAPTER TWO
THE LIFE EXPECTANCY MYTH

"Tell me about Manaboozhou's wife."

"No. No, it doesn't start there. There's way more to it, before he was even born. . . . They lived together for four generations."

"Who did?"

"His parents."

"Whose parents?"

"Manaboozhou's parents."

"They lived together for four generations?"

"Yeah. They were great-great-grandparents."

"Are you sure?"

"Yes, I'm sure."

"But, I've seen in books, Wiinona died young, after giving birth to Manaboozhou."

"Gosh, she took pretty good care of herself. Dying in childbirth is just one of those things. Modern storytellers are dwelling on that mother-died-young-thing for poor Manaboozhou. There's way more to that family than that. Today, Indian storytellers think that our ancestors all died young, because all the Indians they see alive today die young. Their parents died young. Their grandparents died young. That was a result of colonialism. It continues today as a result of racism and abuse. It's true that we have the shortest life span of all Americans today. It's true that I will die younger than you. I haven't had the same job opportunities, the same insurance policies, the same preventive health care.

"But my ancestors? The *manido-og*, those mysterious, marvelous, do-anything, be-anything Indians from the past? They were at the top of the pecking order in their socioeconomic system. They *were* the socioeconomic system. They had the best of everything at their disposal. They had plenty of food, shelter, a large land base upon which to roam and relocate at will. . . . No, they lived a long, long time."

"But . . . but . . . longevity is a modern phenomenon."

"No, it's a modern phenomenon for you guys. We lived forever."

"Are you sure?"

"I am certain."

I sigh. Sometimes talking to her is like beating my head against a wall.

"We didn't eat salt pork and pork rinds. That's commodity food."

"Eskimos ate fat."

"Yeah. We had a word for them, eskimoog—meat eaters. Then the Frenchies frenched up the word: esqui*meaux*. But they needed the fat to keep their internal stoves fired up. We ate that way sometimes, too—when we needed to, seasonally. But as soon as we found out that it was bad for us, we wanted to quit. But you guys wouldn't let us."

"What?"

"You wouldn't let Indians make enough money to eat lean. An awful lot of us have been stuck in places where we can't hunt anymore, so we've got to eat cheap store-bought food. Cheap store-bought food is unhealthy store-bought food. You see any Indians shopping at your local hippy trippy health food store?

"Bush Indians were lucky Indians. At least they had a land base. And they'd've kept it clean, too. You can betchyou that. No wonder Indians are going around telling stories about poor Manaboozhou's-mama-died-young, like a poor thing. All the Indians they see around them don't live as long as the non-Indians around them, and the awful, wretched, dysfunctional truth about how non-Indians treat Indians gets thrown back into their stories, like it was reality . . . like we're *supposed* to die young, like it's genetic, like we're stupid, like it's OK.

"And nothing could be further from the truth. They had a nice place to live, a good set of practical rules to live by, and they lived for a damned long time. "

"Who?"

"*All* of them! All of the spirits, the ancestors, the great-great-aunts and the uncles, the grandparents, and all of their parents. . . . And Manaboozhou's parents specifically. . . . They lived for four generations. They became great-great-grandparents."

"Are you sure?"

"Yes. Don't argue with me about it."

This was going to be a long interview. This would be a tough book to write. After all, who was I to argue with her about Manaboozhou's parents, Wiinona and the West Wind?

THE PRACTICAL SIDE OF BEING MARRIED TO THE WEST WIND

"They had four sons."

"Who?"

"Wiinona and Epanigiishimoog."

"Is he the West Wind?"

"Yes. Very busy fellow."

"Of course."

"Pollen."

"What?"

"Pollen. Most people take it for granted."

"Oh, no. I have allergies."

"Look outside on a warm spring day, and the tips of the cedar trees are all colored in yellow. . . . If you don't have cedars, the spruce and the pines will follow in a few days. The balsam and spruce show it well, too. . . . Pollen. The air is heavy with it. Then, when the trees have had their extremities open and waiting for hours, and their muscles are sore, then the right gust comes along, just the right puff. . . . And then it happens, all at once, in a great yellow cloud, so dense you can't see through it. It only takes a minute. You'll see a little bit more, all the rest of the day, even throughout the next day or so. . . . But most of them at once like that, you have to be looking for it. It's that brief love affair between one whole species of tree and the West Wind."

"They all do it at once?"

"Most of them. There are a few aberrant individuals, a few that are a day or so early or late, or maybe even off by a few hours. But most of them coordinate it. They get heavy. They wait. It's a ritual."

"That's beautiful."

"Yes, it is. And that's why he's so damned busy."

"Who?"

"Epanigiishimoog. Everybody expects him sort of regularly, with the seasons, with the hour. . . ."

"With the hour?"

"Of course. Fishermen. They depend upon the calm of dawn and dusk."

"Does the calm have a name?"

"Sometimes. Sometimes different people and animals are responsible for the calm. It's not so much that we have a name for the calm. We have stories for it. Do you understand?"

"A little bit."

"Being the Wind is a tough job."

"Did he choose it?"

"No more than I chose to be me."

"Don't you have control over who you are?"

"Not completely. I couldn't help being an Indian."

"Don't you *want* to be an Indian?"

"No. And I can't help it when people think I am trash. And I can't help it when people think I can't do anything but Indian stuff, or talk about anything but Indian stuff. . . . Indians, we haven't had much control about a lot of things in our lives around here lately. That's why I like it better in the bush. I have more control in the bush. I know the bush. Less of you there. You guys are so unpredictable. Only now, you've decided that the bush is cool. You've decided that North is cool. So you've been moving up here and subdividing it and driving up the price of the bush, and now I can hardly hang on to my own little corner of the bush any more. And you trespass all over it with your snow machines and your four-wheelers, and you think it's too much bush for one Indian, because you don't have to *live* off of it, and if you did, you'd find out that it's not too much bush for anybody, and if you'd let me have a job, I could live off of a whole lot less bush like you guys, too. But, I wouldn't, 'cause I'd just shrivel up and die. I've come to rely upon the bush. It's a lot more predictable than you guys. Even Epanigiishimoog, even the West Wind, he's more reliable than you.

"He had a lot of work to do. He couldn't stay around and help Wiinona with the boys. Each one was born in a different generation. He was busy. He was away a lot."

"She didn't mind?"

"*Mind?* Heck, she was honored. He was the West Wind, after all."

"After all."

"Storms."

"Storms?"

"Storms. He had storms to deliver.

"Seeds."

"Seeds?"

"Seeds. They're heavy. Takes a darned good wind to carry them for miles and miles, uphill, downhill, around cliffs, through valleys, over lakes. Can't grow just anywhere. They need Epanigiishimoog to deliver enough of them to pretty good places."

"Of course."

"Of course. So she raised the boys herself. But he always came back home, and she was always glad to see him. They were in love. They were *really* in love. They had to be. He was away so often, so busy. . . . When the calm of predawn lasts hours into midmorning, we say that they are embraced in an especially long kiss.

"When the sun is bright, stare off, up there into the lakeside cliffs, and you will see them, like two intertwined great pines. They used to lean back against a cliff close to my house. He took the form of a red pine and she a white pine. His bark was rough, patchy, from hard work. Hers was smooth. Her needles were thinner, softer. But, they kissed so long and hard that he tripped and lost his balance. He hung on her for a moment, and almost pulled her over. Then my husband went out with a chainsaw and untangled them. She was the only one left."

"Is she still there?"

"No. No, she died shortly after Manaboozhou was born."

"When was that?"

"Thousands of years ago, I suppose."

I didn't question Rachel's timing of these events, but I began to question whether or not she saw herself as stationary in time. I began to understand why she said that the generations were so big and overlapping, and how interrelated they all were, she, and her family, and the supernaturals. Supernaturals. I wondered if that word was OK.

"Is supernaturals an adequate word to use?"

"It's OK. We don't have a word for spirit, you know. All of that Great Spirit stuff, that's all just a misalignment of the truth. Our word, *manido*, it just means mystery. You asked me why I don't capitalize 'creator.' Well, it's just not like that. It's not like we were created by a god or anything. No, it's just a great big mystery. We were just some practical invention, or a mistake that's stuck around.

"To say we are created in a god's image, how odd! To make a god that looks like us, now that would be vain, wouldn't it?"

"But you describe Manaboozhou and all of the other 'spirits' like humans."

"Well, yeah, that's what makes them so goofy. They are like us. They are not better than us, and no worse. They are never evil. How can we condemn them for acting normal? We *love* them for acting normal."

"Why do you use the term 'Great Spirit'?"

"It fits from the perspective of the outside world. We can see what you want, and we give it to you—like prisoners, like trained animals, like smart businessmen (but not like Madison Avenue, because we still haven't figured out how to change your minds about what you want). Our number system was originally base five. But we could see that you guys were never going to get the hang of it, so we changed over to base ten."

"Are you sure?"

"Yes, I'm sure. When I was a little kid, I knew some old people who still knew some of the old numbers. They tried to teach them to us, as a novelty—'Hey, you wanna learn something neat?' But we didn't listen to them. So, now the old numbers are gone."

"Old people still used them?"

"No. Nobody still used them. They just knew some of them as a novelty. But look at the numbers. Look at the Ojibwe numbers we use today. See that word there inside of that other word? *Ingo*—that only one, that's what it means. *Ingodwaaswi*—one and a unit. That's what it means."

"One and a unit? What does that mean?"

"Six."

"Six?"

CHAPTER THREE

"One and a unit makes six. Base five to base ten. We did it for survival. Mysteries into spirits. Phenomena into gods. We did it for survival. You guys had no common sense. Believing in spirits and gods that controlled you and shaped you. You guys were hopeless. We had no choice. We had to adapt, rename, hide the truth from you. There was just no way you guys were going to get it right. . . .

CHAPTER FOUR
US VERSUS THEM

I've grown to hate being one of "you guys." I hate that she thinks of me that way. I want to be bigger and better than the "you guys" she speaks of. I did not, at any point in my life, wake up and say, "I think I'll be a racist today."

"No one wakes up and says, 'I think I'm going to be a racist today.' Nobody gets out of bed and says, 'I think I'll promulgate racist stereotypes today.'" I've heard her say these things over and over. She knows it too. She knows I never wanted to be a bad human being. Yet, she makes me feel guilty. "Armchair Racism": she'd invented the term long before she ever began to talk to me. Why did I feel a part of it? "Forgive me the term, 'you guys,'" she'd said. "It comes out of the mouth more naturally than 'dominant culture,' more naturally than 'post-Columbian Eurocentric culture,' more naturally than 'poorly educated, self-serving, lazy,' more naturally than 'culture without a conscience.'" There she was, whipping that dead horse, driving home the point, rephrasing it until she was certain that I understood it. "Do you understand?" she'd asked me over and over. The more I understand, unfortunately, the more I am drawn in.

I have developed a relationship of simultaneous repulsion and attraction. "She wasn't always like this," her daughter had said. "She grew into it, after getting kicked in the teeth so often."

I had been intrigued the first time I had met her. I was working on my doctorate in education at Michigan State University. I'd spent my breaks traveling the state. I was originally from northern California. Michigan was an experience for me, and northern Michigan was especially an experience, because it was so separate from the rest of the country, from the rest of the industrialized, flat, southern part of the state.

It was Rachel who had originally pointed this out to me. "Look at the map," she had said plainly. "See how the northern lower peninsula and the eastern upper peninsula are so separate from the rest of the country? Do you see how isolated they are by water? It doesn't matter that we have electronic communication. People aren't ignorant by virtue of lack of communication. They are racists at home. They tighten their grips on their purses when they see us up close. They whisper into the ears of their closest friends, behind closed doors, the realities of their fears. The Indians, the Blacks, the Mexicans, the coloreds, they will ruin their lives, ruin their property values, ruin everything they have worked for, ruin everything they came here for. . . . Racism is close and in-your-face. These big lakes, they isolate these ends of the peninsulas.

"Do you want to see the most open-minded, progressive parts of this state? Look to the extremities. Look to the places where the peninsulas touch the prairies. But don't look here, to the inner recesses of these peninsulas. This is where hatred lives. This is the Deep South of the North. The Deep South became the Sun Belt. Things are more progressive there. Things have flip-flopped. Welcome to the twenty-first century. Welcome to the era of subtle racism. No crosses burned on front lawns here—well, there was that one black guy from the Coast Guard who was stationed in Traverse City—but they transferred him out. Anyhow, no crosses burned on front lawns here anymore. Just exclusion.

"Do you want to see Indians around here? Go out at four in the morning. No self-respecting store manager would hire an Indian to bag groceries, especially on the day shift. People would complain. They'd blame the Indian every time a can was dented, a bag too heavy, any mistake, because we must be stupid, sneaky, not trustworthy, dirty, bad, really bad. . . .

"*Si quaeris peninsulam amoenam, circumspice.*" I hate it when she speaks Latin. She speaks Latin more than anyone I've ever met.

"If you seek a beautiful peninsula, look about you. It's the state motto."

"What's the significance of this?"

"Maybe it wouldn't be so bad, if it wasn't a bunch of peninsulas. The water-bound places that were hardest to reach, that's where the Indians were left holding out in little villages and bands. We shared this place with a few non-Indian workaholics and some adventurous intellectuals. This place was a haven for intellectuals when I was a kid. The virgin timber was gone, and the free homesteads evaporated, as the soil is mostly sandy and cannot support dense life without the forests. It was a glory day of ghost towns. I was lucky enough to be part of it. There were a few subdivided lakes, where the working-class whites huddled on small lots. The landless poor is how the successful farmers looked upon them. But the rest of it was a healing and recovering wild land.

"So the intellectuals flocked here. Harvard professors, scientists, research physicians, award-winning authors. They used to come over to our house for dinner all the time. They were so open and accepting. They embraced us. That's why so many of us went to college. They threw the doors wide open to us. All they cared about was our intelligence and our sensitivity, not the color of our skins.

"But when we came home from college, things here were worse than the accepted racism of the fifties and sixties. The racism of the eighties and the nineties is the ugliest thing I have ever seen. Their population soared, and they built smaller, more efficient cars, and they stretched out their power lines and their highway system. And they moved up here to get away from the Blacks. They moved up here to be safe. But we already had colored people up here. Us. Indians. And, seasonally, the Mexicans. Whew, boy, and you know that the only thing dirtier than an Indian is a Mexican.

"Imagine how ignorant these poor fools all seemed to us, when we came home from graduate school! We came home from Harvard, Oberlin, Stanford—doctors, lawyers, university instructors, teachers—erudite, more than competent, excelling in our fields. Imagine how damned stupid they all looked to us!

"Imagine how it feels like a kick in the teeth, every time they pass us up for a job. No, we couldn't possibly know how to do anything white. Colored teachers cannot teach white children the things that white children need to know . . . because colored teachers don't know about the things that white people need. White people need larger homes, better views, more than one bathroom, nicer clothes, better food. . . . But Indians, well you know, you guys think Indians don't need much to live on, we're *used* to poverty, we're *used* to less, we're *used* to the status quo.

"Do you see how ignorant, ignorant, *hopeless* you guys seem to us?"

CHAPTER FOUR

I hate being one of "you guys." I hate that she thinks of me that way. Or does she think of me as one of the intellectuals? Am I good enough for her or not? Is she going to let me keep interviewing her or not? Am I going to get a book out of this or not? Am I good enough? Am I going to get the job? I've already put in so much effort, almost as much effort as an Indian getting a college diploma, I find myself thinking. I am beginning to understand. And this frightens me.

CHAPTER FIVE
IF YOU FIND SOMETHING THAT WORKS, STICK WITH IT

I remember the first time I came to her house. I'd already left Michigan. I'd given up hopes of writing about her as part of my doctoral thesis. I'd wisely moved on. Her story, I'd eventually discovered, was bigger than the few pages I'd asked her to give me.

I'd met her at the Museum of Ojibwa Culture, near Mackinack Island. It was a great tourist attraction. The classes offered at the museum were so cheap, and at first I'd thought that what she would have to offer would be cheap, too. That was before I'd found out about the hours of grant writing the museum director had spent to bring her there. It didn't matter if the classes didn't fill up. It didn't matter if the participants wouldn't pay what she was really worth. She was a treasure trove of information. She talked, moved, and demonstrated nonstop. She was a natural teacher, a living museum, an enigma.

I was intrigued by the class on Ojibwe culture and arts, this extension of the museum full of ancient quillwork. But she was more than an extension of the cliches in my mind. She was educated, incredibly well-educated. She was better educated than most people I'd ever met. Here I was, writing my thesis on Indians in education, and there just weren't many books about it. And here she was, spouting statistics from the State Board of Education: "The group with the number one highest unemployment in this state is Native American women, followed by Native American men. . . . We have more college diplomas per capita than any other ethnic group in the state. . . . It is not a problem of lack of education, but a problem of inequality in the job market. . . ." On and on and on, she went. She quoted a chapter from a book on contemporary race issues that had been published by Michigan State University Press only months before: "a faulty study" she had called it, "an attempt by educators to justify their jobs. . . . The study indicated that . . . going to college was good for Native Americans, because so many of them went on to graduate school . . . but it ignored the fact that they had nothing to show for all those years of hard work, no job experience, no life savings, no social security paid into the system." I hadn't learned to recognize her rants yet. Who cared if they didn't collect social security? They were going to spend their lives on welfare anyways, right? She hadn't straightened me out yet. I was a virtual bundle of welfare myths and misconceptions.

Intrigued. I'd been intrigued by her. She was going to be my free lunch, my easy source for reference materials. All I'd wanted from her was a brief description of her experiences with the education system. I'd even written to her, a week later, asking her for that simple bit of information. I'd even included a stamped, self-addressed envelope for her response.

Nine months went by before I heard from her. It's not like I'd asked her for something complicated. She was a typical Indian, I was discovering. She talked a good show at first, but then she got unreliable. I didn't ask much of her. And in turn, I was going to write about the continuing trials and tribulations of her people. I would be one more person that understood. I deserved at least the respect of a response. After all, I was going out of my way to include her in my thesis.

The letter was brief. It was probably the only time in her life she was ever brief. "You wrote and asked me to describe my experiences with the educational system. It would take me hundreds of hours to do that. Were I to put in that sort of massive effort, I suppose I'd expect a doctorate of my own, or at least a copyright on the material. I hope you understand. Perhaps you could present me with a few very specific questions, the responses to which would not require a thesis. Please feel free to call me. I really enjoyed meeting you. Sincerely, . . ."

But the phone calls were futile. I gave up on trying to include her in my thesis, except for a few well-chosen sentences. This, she had insisted, was all I should get out of it. It was, after all, my thesis and not hers.

Then, almost two years later, I'd had the idea to write a book, a children's book about Native American stories, about tricksters. "Oh, no. Don't go there," she'd said, "because we don't have tricksters like you think.

The characters are much more complex than that." And somehow, magically, she had sucked me in, and I wanted to know what she knew and how she knew it. Could I write about her and her relationships to the spirits, I'd asked her, not knowing she'd take me literally, not knowing she couldn't outline all those mythological characters if her life depended upon it, not knowing she'd have me eating the word myth like it was cod liver oil with its gag reflex.

I'd already moved back to California. We were going to do this on the phone. But then, I had an opportunity to go back to Michigan, so why not meet her at her house, get some photos of her and her basket collection, do the anthropologist thing? She'd help me draft a letter outlining the goals of this project, a book with shared copyrights. I'd gotten the go-ahead from my university press. I'd obtained a grant for travel and costs.

The cheapest plane fare brought me to Traverse City on a Sunday. She'd told me that, if I arrived on a Sunday, I couldn't have a very big piece of her, that her whole family was busy with her on weekends. It would be hectic. Her oldest daughter picked me up at the airport and drove me to their house. She didn't talk much. It was windy, and the blocky, rusty little station wagon was buffeted around on the state roads. The girl was barely big enough to clear the steering wheel, and I did not have much confidence that she would be able to keep the car on the road in the event of an especially large gust. I thought about offering to drive, but I didn't want to offend her, and I saw that it was a stick shift.

Shortly after the highway split and we made a sharp turn, she pulled into the parking lot of a grocery store.

"Juice is on sale. My mom gave me money to stock up. I should have bought it before I picked you up, but my little brother peed on the couch. I'm sorry." She slid out of the seat and disappeared into the store. I had declined her invitation to come in and pick out any kind of special food that I liked. I was tired from the flight from California, from shuffling from one end of the Chicago airport to the other, where the tiny commuter planes took off. "Puddle Jumpers," the man in the next seat had explained to me after take-off, as I watched the rough seas of Lake Michigan grow smaller and smaller.

The roads were rough with crusted slush. Things had frozen quite quickly, my child escort had told me. Her name was Stella, and she was a watered-down version of her mother. She was shaped like her, she moved like her, but she would never be quite as tall. The temperature dropped over twenty degrees in an hour and a half yesterday, she had explained. "We had thunderstorms yesterday. Then the rain quit, and it got cold. It was very good for the ice rink." She smiled at me, as though I would understand.

"I live at a low elevation," I explained. "I have to go up into the mountains to see much snow." The roads were becoming like tunnels, narrower, more convoluted, with higher and higher walls of snow piled up at their sides.

"We didn't have much snow here this winter," she said, "until last week." It was the ninth of March. The tiny car had slowed to a crawl on an incredibly steep incline, and the girl downshifted. "Only a certain percentage of the road has to meet legal grade." She looked at me, smiling, trying to calm me. "I'm going into civil engineering. It's one of the worst hills in the county. It's OK. There's nothing up here but farms."

And, when it seemed as though the car had come to almost a complete stop, we topped the hill, and the dense maple forest gave way to flat, open farmland and miles of tidy orchards. She turned into the first driveway, along an elegant row of tall poplars. We lurched from side to side, from this point on, as all semblance of a genuine roadway had instantly disappeared. She guided us between two well-spaced poplars, although I'd had my doubts that she could pull it off. Then we inched past the largest backyard ice rink I had ever seen in my life.

"It's almost half the size of a college rink," the girl was beaming. "My mom says it's a form of mental illness." At last, she'd found something worth talking about.

We stopped without skidding, much to my surprise, within walking distance of one of several large red barns.

"Gotta put the juice in a freezer. Be right back." And out she hopped, again. From between two barns, an immense green tractor emerged with a front load of huge wooden beams. The barnyard had been carefully plowed. The tractor driver, tall, blonde, fair, and sunburned, smiled in the direction of the car and disappeared around another barn. I had never been so close to a tractor before. I'd had no idea they were so loud. The tires were taller than a man, and the machine could have crushed the car easily. He drove within inches of it, as though he was not put out that the child had parked in his pathway.

I looked around at the barnyard. Parked in various locations about its fringes were four more cars identical to the one we were riding in, but in various stages of decomposition from rust. They were all brushed clean of snow and looked well waxed and ready to run. They were all one color, metallic gray. They all said Toyota 4WD on the grill. They looked like soldiers. They matched, like the barns. I would later find out that the tractors all matched, too. "If you find something that works, stick with it," she would later tell me.

Stella flung open the barn door with her foot and emerged with a large basket of golden delicious apples. She set it down in an icy spot, turned and twisted the large metal door handle shut, trotted up to the car, flipped open the tailgate, ran back and grabbed the basket, put it in the back of the car, hopped into her seat, handed me an apple, and bit into her own. The whole time, the wind rocked the stationary car. "Whew! Cold!" She was not a girl of many words.

We skidded back out the dirt road, drove past a white farmhouse, and pulled into another non-road flanked by tall pines. It looked too narrow to drive. But there I could see the brown wooden house, buried in snow drifts. The heat of the day before had caused several feet of snow to slide off the metal roof. It had landed in piles so high that the heaps blocked the windows. A path was shoveled out for the doorway, and next to it, several frozen gallon jugs of milk and what must surely have been the back wheel of a tricycle emerged from the snowbank. It reminded me of remote snowy mountain passes I had driven through in California, and it was hard for me to imagine someone finding comfort in it.

The head of a huge barking dog kept appearing in the window halfway up the door. The metal door was torn and scratched, as though from a great beast.

Rachel opened the door just a crack, obviously wrestling with the animal. "Hi! She'll run right up, sniff you, and it'll be over with, I promise." It was as she had described. I stood frozen until the beast, named Lala, began to wag her tail. Literally, I stood frozen. I was not dressed for the wind. I was dressed for travel.

I followed Lala into the house. I smelled fish when I walked through the door. It was a gentle smell. It was a school-cafeteria-on-Friday smell.

The mudroom was large, and dark, because the windows were blocked by the snow. A long, low bench sat against a wall, and the space underneath was overfilled with boots and shoes of various sizes, in a semiorganized jumble. Above the bench ran a thick shelf the length of the room, almost sagging under the weight of at least a hundred canning jars. They were arranged by color, the tomatoes transitioning into tomato sauce, then peaches, then applesauce, and finally pickled jalapeños. From the under-bracing of the shelf emerged wooden pegs, upon which were hung layer upon layer of coats. They were not organized by size, but rather by season, the lighter, warm weather coats on the bottom layers, with the heaviest coats on top. When Rachel swung the door shut, I turned around to see the behind-the-door space filled with pegs full of scarves and caps. School backpacks tumbled haphazardly off one end of the bench.

The next wall had a woodbin that held a full cord, and above it were shelves that held a good twenty cigar boxes, each carefully labeled in magic marker: "cars insurance," "trucks insurance," "tractors insurance," "tax bills–U.S.," "tax bills–Canada," "tax bills–House-1." . . . My god, I didn't know she actually *owned* anything. . . . I felt instant shame for my stereotype. It was a horribly awkward way to feel after only moments in someone's house. My eyes were wide open, because my mind was suddenly wide open. The ceilings were all of wood, with beams a foot and a half high. The boards of the ceilings were wider than any wood I'd ever seen. From the low end of the slanted mudroom ceiling hung bundles of herbs and heavy bags of onions, some bearing green sprouts.

My suitcase was shuffled through an impeccably well-crafted cedar door into a tiny room lined completely in cedar, from floor to ceiling. It was overflowing with bunkbeds, tables, shelves, and chests, all of cedar, all handcrafted. In the center of the concrete floor was a thick wool Persian carpet strewn with bits of scissored paper and glitter, with an open glue stick lying near its middle. The bunks were loosely made with soft, worn, heavily patched quilts made completely from wool. It was one of the co-ziest rooms I had ever seen, a safe harbor from the vast, snowy landscape I had just been driven through.

I stepped up from the lean-to mudroom into the kitchen, which was really one whole side of the house, separated from the living and sleeping areas by a mere counter. The kitchen was moist and wooden. There were no cupboards. Every pot, pan, cup, and dish was out in the open. Hand-made shelves opened up in great V's from every corner, laden with jar after jar of home-canned food. I'd never seen so many pickles in my life. I'd never seen so many carrots in my life. The colors were staggering, the labels amazing. Wild Cranberry Juice—quart after quart after quart—clear, red, and perfect. Dark Sweet Cherries—pint after pint after pint. I was beginning to sort out the jars by size. I was drawn in: cucumber relish, green beans and ham, pickled beets, spiced tomato juice, catsup, turkey broth. I involuntarily walked past the refrigerator and stared at the next flanking shelf. The bottom three shelves were filled with canned milk. Above that were spices and a few grocery store mixes and condiments, but not enough to fill a grocery sack.

I was guided past the compost bucket and the counter into the living room, which was strewn from furniture leg to furniture leg with what appeared to be unravelled plastic audiotape. "Shshsh—cheap entertainment!" she'd cautioned me, when I began to question it. A teenager, standing behind a well-upholstered antique chair, tilted it forward, dumping a small, grayish-white cat from its cushion, and motioned me to sit in it, next to a large chromed parlor stove.

"Chilly?" Rachel asked, opening a stove door in front of my knees, exposing the red-hot coals. I was transfixed by the fire, rendered immobile by the heat that penetrated my welcoming bones. After a few minutes, she reached into a nicked and battered, but beautiful, wooden box full of logs. She threw several pieces of hardwood on the fire, then pushed the stove door all but a half an inch shut, using a small metal tool she seemed to be keeping within inches of her hand at all times. She'd been asking me about my trip, I am sure, although I could not remember a thing I had said to her. I had never witnessed the things I was seeing in the quantity in which I was seeing them, and I was beginning to feel very small. . . . Then the logs burst into flames, and after a few moments, she speedily clamped the door shut with the metal tool. Letting me sit there, with the stove door open, was a special treat, I would eventually learn, a reward for a long trip or a long, bone-chilling job out-of-doors. I would later feel ashamed that it had been squandered on me that first day, merely because I was not used to the climate.

I looked up and rotated my head slightly to the right, only to be confronted by another wallfull of massive shelves full of canning jars—more, different things, things sorted by type: juices, fruits, jams, wild mushrooms, beans, beans, beans, pickles, pickles, pickles, pie fill, pie fill, pie fill.

A large crocheted afghan with a single huge butterfly motif lay on the polished floor boards between our feet. The cat had curled up on it. She was runt-sized, not quite white, and not quite gray. She had soft, beige, barely discernable tabby stripes on her whitish body, but her head and ears wanted to be soft gray like a Persian. The tail was strictly dark gray tabby. "She got it at a garage sale," Rachel would eventually say. The cat looked up at me briefly, and I saw that its eyes were round, blue, and beautiful. Rachel had seen me staring at the cat. "She tried her darnedest to be beautiful, but some things just don't work out," she said.

The house was full. Things were piled on top of things. On top of the shelves of canning jars were shelves of board games. On top of the woodstove was a steaming porcelain pot of water (to humidify the air, so it would hold more heat, I was eventually informed) and some large, preheated cast iron skillets. On top of the skillets was perched a lipped cookie sheet full of fried smelt.

"I didn't know you had smelt here."

"Oh yeah, they were first introduced into the big lake my family has a house on, about twenty minutes south of here, just across the county line. Back then, people didn't seem to understand how sneaky a fish could be. The little guys moved down the drainage crick into Lake Michigan, and they just spread out over all of the Great Lakes. These are from Lake Superior. Uncle Bill's got a house on the Indian River, just above where it empties out into the big pond there." She pronounced the word Indian *Inny-un*, with extra stress on the "I," like it was a private word that belonged to Indians and not whites.

She was off on a long one. I drifted back into the story of the smelt: "He's got this trapdoor in his floor. You hop out of bed at midnight, lift it up, run down the stairs, open the big door onto the river and dip. Big poles. We've got metal mesh nets on big, long poles. You can feel 'em thumpin' right into the net, and then you flip 'em into the bucket. You don't even get your feet wet." She was animated then, rising up out of her seat as she spoke. The tiny cat stirred and readjusted.

"My brother still lives down there on the six forty."

"Six forty?"

"Acres."

"Forty-six acres?"

"Six hundred and forty acres," she said slowly, deliberately. I felt a fool. She didn't have much respect for anybody who lived on fewer than eighty acres, I would someday learn. She considered us the landless poor, "the ignorant of the mortgaged nonwealth" as she referred to us, the two-acre lot dwellers.

"It's the greatest feeling in the world," she said, "to just scoop food up out of the river like that."

Then she burst into song, in Ojibwe. It was smooth and rhythmic. It *sounded* fun. It was at that point that I realized that two girls, perhaps eleven and twelve, had been sitting on a wooden wall bench behind me, hanging on my every word. In fact, the room seemed to be full of children, or at least their accoutrements. A six-year-old with an immense gap in lieu of a front tooth was dancing sideways past me, hips wagging in time to the song, waving two balled-up wads of audiotape in his clenched fists. He thrust out the wads like pom-poms, silently mouthing the words to unknown football cheers in Ojibwe. He was blondish and dark-skinned, obviously the product of Rachel and the tractor driver from the barns. Of the two girls behind me, only one appeared to be part Indian. The taller and younger-looking of the two was willowy and had the potential to become a fashion model when she grew up. The darker girl sat stone still, watching her mother sing, while the willowy one freely rocked back and forth, singing along in Ojibwe.

"It's the Smelt Dipping Song!" sang out Rachel, and she repeated the verses, demonstrating the motions. She overemphasized certain syllables to the point of absurdity, and even the dark girl laughed. Stella hummed about the kitchen, like a well-oiled machine, leaving a swath of dirty dishes in her path. Her socks hung halfway past her toes, and a fluffy ball of black dog fur stuck to the end of one, as she shuffled along the smooth wooden floor, oblivious to the fact that she might be anything less than beautiful. Stella was definitely at peace with herself.

"When I was little, we used to seine for minnows. . . ." Rachel began. "It was a big, flat, fine, rectangular net, set up on two sapling poles. We'd work it, one on each side, following the schools of minnows. We'd scoop them up with a big swoop, then dump them into the pail. Half of them would get away. Then we'd take them back up to the house, make sure there were no sticks or rocks in with the fish, shake 'em in a bag of flour, then fry 'em up whole. Little eyeballs looking up at you and everything. We used to make our own flour tortillas, even up in the bush. We called them piigiiganh—flat breads—and my dad loved jalapeños, and we canned them for him. And we just filled a warm tortilla with those little feeshies, eyeballs and guts and all, and we'd throw the jalapeños on top of them."

She stopped and smiled directly at me, as though describing eating minnows, guts and all, was like describing a Christmas morning. I stared at the heaping cookie sheet full of smelt, slowly reheating on the woodstove. At least I knew a little something about smelt. They were small fish, no bigger than ten inches, but each one was cleaned with scissors and its head and intestines removed.

"Somebody bring me a cup of tea!" she called out.

"Do it yourself," Stella responded, munching on what was perhaps her third apple.

"Can't. Kitty's toenail is stuck in my sock."

"Awww . . ." Stella looked over.

"She's so rarely this relaxed," Rachel commented. Then the six-year-old pom-pom boy danced by again, shaking the whole wooden floor. The cat cocked its head and opened one eye wide. I could certainly understand why it would have to keep its guard up.

"*In gii piin dam an chii giitchii. . . .*" Willowy Girl began to sing again in Ojibwe. Her name was Zoey.

Rachel translated the song: "I just hauled in a really big mess of teeny weeny fish. . . ." She swayed when she sang it. The children all laughed like there was a big joke I didn't get.

"Is it time for me to take my medicine?" Zoey asked.

"Well, I dunno—is it?" Rachel responded.

The girl rambled off a series of times.

"Stella, take the Divine Miz Z to her house to get her meds," Rachel instructed.

"Later."

"Now."

"You go with them. You'll enjoy the ride." She spoke to me like one of the children, barely glancing up at me, while she shook the cat free from her sock. "I'll have dinner ready when you come back."

I didn't want to ride anywhere. I didn't want to see any more roadside walls of snow. But I was obedient. I could see that I was a small part of her day.

For all that Stella was quiet, Zoey was not. She asked me question after question about myself. "My real mother died when I was three," she announced to me matter-of-factly. The drive took about twenty minutes one way, and the girl had managed to inform me that her natural mother had died when she was three at least half a dozen times.

"Gee, what's that you say, Z, did your momma die when you were three? Geez, give the ol' wicked stepmother a break will ya. Like she's gotta be some kind of a saint or something to compete with a crappy old ghost!" Stella spoke the only tirade I would ever hear her utter, and the younger girl sat sullenly as the Tercel crawled and was downshifted on the increasingly steep hill. We were entering a subdivision of two-acre lots full of half-million-dollar homes. ("The Wallboard People"—Rachel would eventually share the moniker with me.)

The house we drove up to was three stories tall, with a turret and an observatory and a radio tower on top. We parked next to a silver Lexus. Stella went in with Zoey, and the two girls quickly emerged with three medicine bottles and a bag of miniature Mounds candy bars. The bag was half empty by the time we got back home again. Stella had turned the radio on a bit too loud, effectively eliminating any further possibility for conversation. I noticed that the gray dashboard of the Tercel had a big #4 scrawled on it in magic marker. I realized I was riding in a fleet car.

CHAPTER SIX
MAPLE SYRUP

"A re you spending the weekend?" I asked Zoey, as she followed me into the house and to my chair.

"No, I just sort of live here sometimes," said the Willowy Miz Z.

It was only two o'clock in the afternoon. The small, golden, splayed smelt were beginning to sizzle on the woodstove. I realized that all I had had on the plane was a bag of pretzels. That was long before Chicago.

Dinner was not ready when we came back, as Rachel had promised. She was plunging the toilet. She bolted down to the mudroom for a gallon of bleach, ran back into the bathroom, and kept plunging. The Toothless One was also pantless, but he still clung to the makeshift pom-poms. I could hear Rachel flushing and rinsing something in the bathtub. There was a rush of bleach in the warm air, then more rinsing. She bolted back to the mudroom with the bleach, pulled off her hooded sweatshirt, and threw it in the washing machine. She stood in a shirtlike sports bra, in front of the sink, and washed her hands and arms up to the elbows with LAVA soap. Twice. I noticed that she looked a lot slimmer without the hooded sweatshirt. She didn't look forty-six. She looked thirty-six.

She darted into the bedroom, past a waist-high black ash woven hamper, a museum-quality piece, no doubt full of dirty little socks. She emerged in a clean, smooth hooded sweatshirt. It was just like the other one—same size, same brand, same style, different color.

"Poo—ya gotta treat it like pesticides," she explained sheepishly, smoothing down the fresh sweatshirt. I looked out the back window, into the orchard that stretched back a full half mile from the house. I knew then that she did know about pesticides, that she did know about whole worlds of things I'd never thought to give her credit for. There it was, that guilt, creeping in again, accompanied by a feeling of total ignorance. I hadn't observed her lifestyle close up for more than a few hours, and already I was feeling that my own lifetime full of experiences was tiny and inadequate. Stockholm syndrome, I told myself. They're holding me captive, these bizarre children.

"Give that tray of fish a shake." Rachel looked in my direction. The children had all disappeared, like magic.

"Do you have a potholder?" I asked. And she breezed over, smiling, pulled the long sleeves of the sweatshirt down over her hands, and gave the tray a quick shake, flipping a few of the little fish into the air.

She grabbed a small pot off the kitchen wall. Then she swept two pint jars of carrots off a shelf flanking the refrigerator and placed them on the electric stove. She pulled out a metal bottle opener from a plastic key coil on the belt loop of her blue jeans and popped open the jar lids. She very unceremoniously dumped the carrots into the pot and flipped the stove burner onto high. She pulled a heavy quart jar of applesauce from the never-emptying shelves, as though pulling a rabbit out of a hat. She pulled out the bottle opener, a "church key" she called it, popped the lid off of the jar and left it on the counter with a big spoon. Snap! The church key returned to her waist. A half pint of pickled jalapeños. Snap! The church key disappeared under the sweatshirt.

"Find me a lemon or a lime, please." She pointed to the refrigerator. "Either in the door or the bottom drawer."

I found a half lime in the door of the fridge, but it looked small, so I opened the drawer and rummaged under the leaf lettuce until I found a whole lemon. She cut them up with godspeed.

The entire bottom shelf of the refrigerator, above the drawer, was filled with quart canning jars full of brown liquid. I'd counted four rows, three deep. "What is that?" I had asked.

"Maple Surple."

"Oh."

"We don't have a word for it."

"Oh."

"Sugar."

"What?"

"Sugar. We have a word for maple sugar."

"Oh."

"And the sap."

"Uh huh."

"But not for syrup. We didn't make syrup. We didn't have glass jars."

She stood there staring at me, twirling the church key on its red spiral umbilical cord. I was fairly certain she was trying not to laugh.

CHAPTER SEVEN
JAM

Rachel was calm and relaxed, as she stood outlined against the open refrigerator, sipping peach juice from a quart jar of canned fruit, the same way most of us would drink milk out of the carton when no one is looking. She was sexy and confident when she was cooking. It was the first time, in the two hours since I'd arrived, that she'd looked me in the eye.

Willowy Zoey stumbled up the mudroom steps into the kitchen with the other girl her age, whom I'd come to realize was, except for that brief drive for medications, attached to her at the hip. (Rachel would refer to them as the conjoined twins.) "Can I have a cookie?" asked Zoey.

"No." And the two girls tumbled into the two chairs Rachel and I had previously occupied by the woodstove. They stared at me, unabashedly. I smiled back. The middle girl was named Isabel, I eventually figured out. She was lighter than my driver, Stella, and, although at least four years younger, a good inch taller. She would be a shadow of her mother, or so I'd thought, until I'd met the father.

Rachel sawed through a roundish loaf of hard-crusted high-quality whole grain bakery bread. Stella popped up the steps, took one last bite from an apple core, and dropped it into the compost bucket. She looked at her mother expectantly.

"Stells Bells, look for an open jam," Rachel instructed.

Stella practically disappeared face first into the refrigerator. From within its yellowish glow, she barked out, "Z! Jam! Now!"

Zoey stumbled again, merely trying to untangle her gangly limbs, unfolding from the upholstery and wood like a spider. She tripped past the hot woodstove to the imposing wooden shelves at the end of the room. From her knees, she called out the possibilities:

"Mmmm, plum jam!" called out Zoey.

"Mmmm," said Rachel.

"No," said Stella.

"Die first," said Isabel.

"Wild blueberry," called out Zoey.

"Sick of it," said Stella.

"Strawberry?"

"Wild or regular?"

Zoey tipped the canning jar upside down and shook it, peering at it through thick glasses. "Uh, regular, I think."

"Nah."

"Sauerkraut," announced Zoey.

"Mmmm, Mom, can I open a package of hot dogs?"

"No, Stella."

"But Moo-om! I hate fish!"

"You'd hate your own butt, if it wasn't attached."

"Cherry."

"Hate cherries," said the toothless one. He was still for the first time since I'd arrived.

"Wild blackberry."

"Not bad, Zoe. Think you picked a winner."

"Mmmm . . . wild blackberry peach." Zoey hopped up, ignoring their preferences.

"Dad won't eat it."

"Screw Dad."

Zoey ceremoniously tapped the jar's gold colored band with a silver spoon handle. She did this with her head cocked, as though she were tuning a piano. Apparently, the only jars that had bands over the lids were the ones whose bands were stuck. After opening the band, with what I saw to be uncanny strength for such an uncoordinated child, Zoey reached under the front of Rachel's shirt and found the church key. The jar opened with a dull thud, as the suction was broken. Rachel began to move across the room, and the red plastic coil stretched out several feet, before the church key was pulled from Zoey's unconscious hand. It hit Rachel in the back of the calf before retreating to her waist. She withdrew her hands into her sleeves, shook the smelt, and announced: "Eat."

I stood with my back to the woodstove, well out of the way, as the children grabbed their own plates off a shelf and shuffled from woodstove to cookstove, filling them with food. The bread was semifrozen, so Isabel and Zoey had created an assembly line manufacturing dense toast, heavy with margarine and succulent jam that held its shape in spooned heaps. The kids pronounced it *margareen*, with a strong accent on the last syllable, and sometimes as *margareeney*, with an extra syllable. Through it all, they managed to dole out milk and food to the littlest child.

They spread out all over the living room and around the woodstove. The heavy black walnut dining table was covered with mail and bowls of porcupine quills sorted out by size and color. Rachel ate standing up, occasionally helping the six-year-old who held the seat of honor, a tall caned barstool at the well-lit kitchen counter. Luminescent, flat Halloween skeletons dressed in small black frocks were propped up in the other bar stools around the living room. They seemed to be out of commission, and no one dared move them.

The conjoined twins stared at me while I ate. They had both heaped pickled jalapeños on top of the crispy smelt. Each large, dark blue plate held a pool of applesauce with carrots in the middle. Periodically, each of them would swirl a smelt in the applesauce, then eat it, like a french fry. Smelt are so small that they are eaten bones and all. I was informed that they were members of the trout family, which is why their scales and skins were edible too. Zoey announced that she couldn't chew the bones very well and proceeded to remove the rubber bands from her braces. She laid them in her plate, at the edge of her applesauce.

When fixing my own plate, I'd noticed that no one put margarine on their vegetables, so I followed suit. The carrots were surprisingly sweet.

Shortly after we finished eating, Rachel's husband came back from the barns. He unzipped each leg of his overalls, from ankle to thigh, before stepping out of them. Then he removed his immense insulated boots. He spoke to no one. No one spoke to him. He disappeared into the bathroom for several minutes, then emerged in long johns, freshly washed and smiling. His family crowded around him, smiling, and all of them, *all* of them, Zoey included, huddled together with their arms around each other, kissing and making smoochie noises. The dog went crazy, and they all laughed and kissed at the dog.

I was introduced to Tall Man Jack, not that tall really, perhaps six feet or six-foot-one. He was less imposing, now that the layers of clothing were peeled off. He had little to say to me. Ah, that's where Stella gets it, I thought.

"Has everyone eaten?" Jack asked.

"Yes."

So the man emptied all of the food containers onto his plate. He shook garlic salt over the whole thing, applesauce and all, sat down on the couch, and turned on the TV.

"Go outside and move the dish." He spoke in the direction of the three girls. They grumbled, then donned coats and boots.

"Take a broom with you!" Jack called out.

I watched in disbelief out the window, as the three teenagers waded through knee-deep snow to a large satellite dish. Zoey, the tallest, swept its surface clean, falling backwards repeatedly in the deep snow. Finally, Isabel and Zoey hung in various positions on the big black dish, while Stella gave hand signals from the back of the machinery. Jack manned the remote control and gave Rachel instructions as to the cardinal directions. Rachel in turn relayed the information out an open window from her knees, on top of a king-sized bed against the wall on the far side of the room. The cold air traveled the length of the room and settled at my feet.

"OK!" The window was shut, and the girls returned, spewing wet boots and clothing and chunks of snow. The dog was ordered to stay in the mudroom, until her paws melted. I was forced to move away from the woodstove, as boots and clothing were hung from the chairs and piled around it to dry.

All of this work was for The Weather Channel.

"Good day to flood the ice rink. Start now, and you could get in at least two good floodings, with a freeze period in between. It's going to be cold and clear for several days." Jack was directing his hopeful instructions to the girls, but they moaned. He ended up playing an endless game of Uno with all of the children before bundling up and trudging back to his barns.

Rachel was constantly in motion. None of her moves were wasted. She was a multitasker. Each time she took a jar lid to the recycling bins in the mudroom, she returned up the steps with an armload of firewood for the smaller wood box near the stove. A pile of clean laundry sat in a corner of the kitchen space, near its juncture with a bedroom and the mudroom. Each time she went into the bathroom, she dipped down and grabbed a towel or a washcloth, folding it along the way. Each time she glided into a bedroom, she grabbed a shirt, two socks, or several pairs of underwear. I could see that I would have no piece of her today. I knew I would glean the most information by merely watching.

"Zoey," Rachel called out. "Come get your rubber bands out of my compost."

CHAPTER EIGHT

THE SOCK PILE FROM HELL

It was the largest bathroom I had ever seen in my life, and none of them, except for Tall Man Jack, closed the door when they used it. It was as though they all lived in one giant open space and skittered around one another, like marbles being shaken in a frying pan.

The bathroom was all wood—beautiful, beautiful wood. Ceiling of wood, floor, walls, rows and rows of wooden pegs—all draped with big, colorful beach towels in various stages of drying. It was a system I had to be taught—Jack's system, Rachel had informed me. "He's anal retentive," she'd said, lovingly, as she stood in front of a tall series of shelves full of canned goods. Her head was haloed by what were surely at least a hundred quart jars of applesauce. They were quite a pair. The towels were rotated in a counterclockwise direction along the pegs, I was told. When I came out of the shower, I was to use the towel closest to the tub. I was to put the wet towel on the peg farthest from the tub, and then move all the other towels up in progression. By the time a towel made its way back to the tub, it would be dry enough to use again. They didn't seem to mind that a stranger was about to enter into the towel rotation. I sort of liked it. I thought about Zoey and the big hug.

The inner shower curtain was clear plastic, decorated with cerulean blue hand- and footprints of various sizes, heavily smudged and overlapping. I realized what a fun time it must have been, all of them dipping themselves into the acrylic paint and crawling over the shower curtain all at once. I could see how each of them must have felt a sense of warmth and belonging each time they showered. Still, I was annoyed by the endless supply of bottles of girlie shampoos, conditioners, and creme rinses that repeatedly fell from the tub wall onto my toes. I wondered how Jack put up with it.

I stuck just one hand from the warmth of the tub stall, beyond the double curtains, quickly pulled in the big towel, then dried off before stepping out into the cool room. I thought about wiping the water droplets off the inside of the shower, as my mother had taught me. But a glance around at the layers of white lime told me that no one else had bothered in a long, long time. I pulled back the curtains, prepared to exit onto a thick bath mat, only to discover that the big black dog was curled up on the mat. She was awake, but seemed unwilling to move. I looked the length of the room. The door was shut. I don't know how the dog got in there with me. I had to straddle her to step out from the slick, wet bathtub, hanging by both hands from the two wooden pegs closest to the shower. They didn't give a bit, as I swung my full weight out over the dog. Her eyes followed me, as I wiped my wet footprints off the wooden floor.

I am neither lithe, nor lanky as my hosts, so I keep my limbs well lubed with baby powder when I exit from bathing. This, I discovered, would be a huge mistake. Within the hour of my exit from the bathroom, several wooly-socked children would be sliding across the shiny floorboards, at first by accident, and then on purpose. Much to my horror, they perfected it into an art form. At Rachel's urging, they gathered up every pillow in the house and piled it on the far side of the bathroom across from the door. Then they took a running start from the kitchen and skidded into the opposite wall. They begged me for more baby powder.

"Enough, enough!" Rachel shrieked, when Isabel began shaking the bottle vehemently. "You'll get it all over the house, then these floors will be a death trap!"

After they tired of it, they began wandering around the house, leaving treacherous little white sock prints.

"Change socks, everybody, now!" Rachel commanded. She followed them around with wet rags, cleaning up the baby powder. She slowly mopped the kitchen floor, working her way into the bathroom, frequently tossing saturated rags into the garbage. I felt horribly guilty, and I joined her on my knees, wiping. After we finished, the children were ordered to redistribute the pillows. They were all brought into the living room, piled into a heap on top of an eight-foot-long oval rag rug, and jumped upon, repeatedly. Eventually, they were redistributed in a haphazard fashion into every corner of the house, and the children were ordered out to the barns to flood the ice rink.

I had thought that I would finally be able to spend quiet time with Rachel. But she emerged from her bedroom with two Xerox paper boxes full of mismatched socks, dumped them onto the king-sized bed in the living room corner, and hopped up to sort socks. At least she was stationary for a while. For Rachel, this *was* quiet time.

"Sorting the Sock Pile from Hell" is how she described what she was doing. She lined them up in long rows, by color, then into subsets by length, then into subsets by cuff type. Surprisingly, the pairs began to match up quickly. She folded them into one another and tossed them into one of the paper boxes.

"The matching socks may show up in the laundry months apart," she explained. Several were magic markered with matching designs and letters of the alphabet, to help her sort them out. I noticed several with a big Z, for Zoey. It *was* a quiet time, and I got to reaquaint myself with Rachel a little bit, to remember why I liked her.

It didn't surprise me that she had a bathroom the size of a small mobile home. Everything about her was immense, even the unmatched sock pile, and especially the satisfaction she received by cutting its volume by two-thirds.

CHAPTER NINE
NO REST FOR THE WICKED

By the time the girls returned from the barns and began spewing snow-encrusted clothing, Rachel had manufactured a huge fruit salad with chunks of apple, orange, and various frozen and canned fruits. The whole thing was cemented with whipped nondairy topping and shredded coconut. I was amazed at the endless variety she pulled out of freezer bags and jars. The fruit salad was supper, along with more of the good bread and a slab of Gruyère cheese.

Rachel had developed a taste for the rich, strong cheese when she was a student in Switzerland. "There are a lot of doors open to smart people," she said, "until they come home and turn back into niggers again." When she described eating lunch at Thornton Wilder's house, I believed her. When she described posing for photos in a leather miniskirt in front of the art nouveau entryway to the subway station at Guy Moquet, I believed her, even before Stella produced the leather miniskirt, held it up, and said, "Look, it won't even fit me." It was easy to imagine Rachel as lithe and beautiful, turning heads on the streets of Paris. She was graying at the temples, now, and she looked sort of worn out, but she was still pretty.

She only wore one brand of blue jeans. She bought them on sale, four or eight at a time. She hated shopping. She wore one style of watch, a simple, old-fashioned, gold-colored Timex. It was just like the first watch she had ever had, the one her high school English teacher had bought her. She and the teacher had remained friends until the old woman's death some years before. Rachel couldn't bring herself to wear another watch. She was so verbal, she must have been an English teacher's dream, back in the days when people taught English because they liked it.

She made her coffee in a percolator, at least half decaf and very weak, but always the best coffee. She loved the taste, but the caffeine kept her awake, even if the coffee was decaffeinated. She drank it half and half with canned milk and switched to hot peppermint tea with canned milk after ten in the morning. She brewed big pots of the tea every few days and stored quart jars of it in the refrigerator or outside on the doorstep.

She was a woman of routine. She was a woman of measured caution. "Indians get kicked in the teeth if they try anything new," she would say. I knew I was supposed to understand it, but I didn't. I interpreted it as paranoia, which was really absurd, the more I'd thought about it. As a basketmaker and an artist, Rachel was known for pushing boundaries. During that week at her house, I listened to her side of a conversation in which she'd turned down a job. A woman from a social service agency had obtained a grant to provide programs that empowered teenage girls. The girls had told the woman that they wanted a workshop on dreamcatchers. "No, no, dreamcatchers are too Buckwheat!" Rachel told the woman. "They weren't telling you they wanted dreamcatchers, they only used that word because it's the only Indian concept they could verbalize." But no matter how much Rachel tried to talk the woman into a more racially progressive alternative, the more adamant the woman became. "The girls said they wanted dreamcatchers, and we're going to give them dreamcatchers because it will empower them if we give them what they asked for," insisted the woman.

"Well, it's a good thing they didn't tell you they wanted to go out broomsticking niggers!" Rachel announced, "or you' be offering me twenty bucks right now to walk down the side of the road."

"Good for you Mom!" Stella announced. "Don't do anything you're not comfortable with."

"Mmm-hmm," Rachel nodded. "Woke up this morning and said, 'Think I'll promulgate a few damaging racial stereotypes today.'"

She pulled up the hood on her sweatshirt and headed out the door with the compost bucket. She wasn't wearing a coat. She was wearing tennis shoes. No, no, she wasn't exactly cautious in the way I would be. But she was cautious in other ways. She was cautious not to let herself be used by other people as a free and easy ride. Wasn't that what I was doing here? God, I hated this woman!

I hated her even more when she coerced me into borrowing warm clothes and going out to flood the ice rink one more time.

The boots were overly large, rounder and funnier-looking than anything I'd ever imagined myself wearing. There was room for two pairs of socks and then some. "Don't want 'em tight," she'd said. "Dead air space between the boot and the toes is a good insulator."

I don't think I'd ever worn so many clothes before. And I hadn't worn mittens since I was a child. "Warmer than gloves!" she'd insisted. I waddled out the door after her, past the comforting glow of the porch light, around the back of the house into almost darkness. We stumbled through a path in the woods, made by a tire from the big tractor. I lurched at almost every step. The path was deeply rounded from the tractor tire. I did not know it at the time, but tractor tires are filled with fluid and are designed to leave minimal impact on the surface they pass over. Eventually dim lights appeared in the distance, just as Rachel in front of me veered sharply to the left. I saw eery, fleeting images of naked tree branches at eye level, just before the light disappeared.

"Sorry. Should've brought a flashlight," Rachel said. "I can do this in my sleep."

We emerged from under giant, twisted trees to the area in front of the barns where Stella had brought me earlier. Rachel pushed me into the barn, where I stood stupidly and blinked. The first thing I saw was a giant moosehead mount, covered in sawdust. Below it was a clock. Six p.m. I realized it was time to be hungry. I walked over to a barn stall that contained a half dozen baskets of apples, wiped the sawdust off one, and began to eat it. I could hardly think. The screeching sounds that came from the back room of the barn were deafening. I peeked in the open door. Jack was pushing heavy boards through a loud machine. He wore safety glasses and what must have been industrial ear muffs. He did not notice me.

Rachel began to pull a large, heavy rubber hose from its concentric rings on a wall rack next to a raging woodstove. She lined up stretches of the hose in long loops, side by side on the concrete floor of the barn. Then she opened the barn door, leaped out, and pulled the hose across the snow and disappeared into the dark. She ran back, flipped the faucet end of the hose out of the barn, and shut the door. She disappeared into the dark again, and then the barnyard lit up like daylight. She ducked into another barn, and the other end of the ice rink was illuminated. She pointed to a metal faucet barely protruding from a snowbank and hollered at me to pick up my end and screw it into the faucet.

"Work fast before the hose freezes!" she called out, smiling. "Groundwater is warm stuff tonight!"

She stood expectantly at a distant corner of the rink. "Turn it on!" I was surprised at how long it took for water to finally come out of the hose. Rachel immediately began to dance back and forth in a regular pattern, putting water on the rink. I waved goodbye and turned to go back into the warm barn.

"Uh uh!" she shouted. "Hose man!"

"What?"

"Hose man. Gotta have a hose man. It's freezing fast. The hose will leave humps."

I hated her even more at that moment.

CHAPTER TEN
FLOODING THE ICE RINK

L ala watched us, curled up in the snow off to one side of the ice rink. I could see her eyes reflecting the floodlights, as we swept back and forth, from one side of the rink to the other, inching down the rectangle. The pace was slow. There was a little bit of a wind, and I found myself working backwards, when I could, to keep the wind off my face. I began to understand why Rachel had insisted that I wear something with an attached hood that would leave no wind gap at the back of my neck.

"People think of the Ojibwe as dressing in loincloths and in loose buckskin without anything but a feather or two on our heads. Not so. We dressed more like the Inuit a good part of the year."

Inuit. I was glad that she used that word. She was so old-fashioned, that I thought she might use Eskimo again. Even the term "Indian" seemed antiquated to me. People were saying "Native American." Why wasn't Rachel?

"We wore hats that fit over our whole heads like heavy skullcaps," she said, "with big ol' ear flaps. Kind of like *this*." She pulled back her windbreaker hood. The hat was pale blue, brown, and white, sort of Mongolian-looking, with a pom-pom on top.

"Did you make that hat?"

"Naw. Probably Mongolian—maybe Peru. Warm as heck though. Ugly, isn't it?" The chin ties wiggled when she talked. The hat framed her face in such a way that it made her look a full twenty pounds heavier. It took guts to wear a hat like that. But this wasn't exactly a public setting.

I would come to learn her public-versus-private clothing categorization system. Public clothing was used only for going out in public, and it was donned only moments before leaving. The same was true of children's school clothes. Clothing was downgraded as it became faded or stained. Some things were OK for the grocery store, for visiting other farmers, or for going to the doctor ("He sees you naked anyways").

"Washing wears stuff out," she'd tell the kids. "Think before you do it." The exception to this was the six-year-old's clothing. After school he was disrobed in the mudroom, and his clothing dumped directly into the washing machine. "For sanitation purposes," she would explain, while he washed his face and hands in the deep sink. A squirt gun filled with liquid hand soap sat in a small plastic bowl in a corner of the sink, just for this ritual. At least she tried to keep it entertaining.

"One thing you learn about living in the bush is germs," she began.

"Germs?"

"Yeah, germs."

"Because you can't wash?"

"No. That's the stupidist thing I've ever heard."

"Then what?"

"Other people."

"Other people in the bush?"

"Tourists."

"Tourists?"

"Tourists. They bring in new germs. We use up all our own germs, let the colds and the flus run right through the whole family, and there we are healthy as can be, for weeks on end. Then we go for a walk on one of the tourist trails in the park. We end up getting sick. The handholds are worn smooth on the trees along the trail. . . . You know you're just picking up germs every time you touch them, but you need them not to fall over. And you wash as soon as you can, but by then you've touched your eye or you've wiped your own nose. Mostly intestinal stuff, that's what we get. People must think that because they're out in the wilds, they can forget about sanitation."

"Tell me more about the old-style clothing."

"Nothing much to tell. Warm, practical, fur-lined to keep snow and wind out. Mittens had big cuffs. Still do today." She extended a mittened arm. Red plaid polyester—halfway up to the elbows. She always managed to make me lose my bearings in time. Here she was wearing commercially reproduced clothing, using it to demonstrate traditional Ojibwe clothing. It didn't seem right.

"Did the Ojibwe have buttons?"

"Nah, we invented Velcro. Haven't you heard of the American Indian Science and Engineering Society?"

"Is there really such a thing?"

"Math and science are color-blind."

"Tell me more about the clothing."

"Don't know much about it."

She knew more about it than most people. She was just holding back.

"Do you want to take a turn?" She turned the hose in my direction, watering the toe tops of my immense boots.

I did. I really did. After watching for several minutes, I'd come to find it interesting, in a strange way. The ice was so slick from the previous flooding, that it was hard to walk. I had to shuffle. I didn't dare completely lift a foot. If I accidentally stepped into the flooding water, I welcomed the stabilizing stickiness as each boot momentarily froze to the ice. It was hard to see where I had flooded, because of the angle of the light. It had been easier to see when I was off to the side, holding up the hose for Rachel. I had been able to tell her whenever she missed a spot.

Flooding the rink was nothing like what I had expected. I had thought that we would simply turn the fat hose onto the rink and let an inch or so of water out within the retaining banks. But it wasn't like that at all. We were adding to the rink only a fraction of an inch at a time, except in the low spots, where the water puddled. Those spots tended to harbor air bubbles, and we had to break into them with the heels of our boots to get them to fill up with water. "An air bubble is a death trap," she had said, and I would eventually learn that it was a place for a skate blade to break through, creating drag and perhaps a bone-crushing fall.

I waddled back and forth across the rink the "short" way, perhaps a hundred and ten feet, waving the hose in front of me, the width of my arm sweep. It was a comfortable sweep, and I had to make sure to keep the end of the hose only an inch or so from the surface. Otherwise it would splatter. As I worked, I was surprised to see a glaze forming on the zippered cuffs of my snow pants. Being the water man was a lot warmer than being the hose man, I found out, because I was swaying back and forth constantly. The hose man just waited a few feet away and then shuffled forward to stay level with the water man. The hose man also had to keep the hose out of the way and to keep moving it so that it did not freeze to the rink or cause a slush ridge. This was incredibly difficult and required a lot of bending, which was not easy deep inside so many layers of clothing. Every time I bent, the snap popped at my waist, and I had to drop the hose to take off my mittens to fix it. Then I had to pick up the hose again. It was a vicious cycle. Rachel was very good at whipping the hose around, getting the kinks out from a distance. Several times when I was the hose man, I let kinks form, causing the water flow to slow to a trickle. At this temperature, the hose would develop a predisposition for kinks in the same places over and over, she had explained, so kinks were a very bad thing. I came to recognize the cycles of the pump and the pressure tank. Just when I would find myself staring down at the unflooded two-thirds of the ice mass, thinking what a snail-like procedure it was, the pump would kick in, and I could move more quickly again. It was fun. It was really fun. I liked looking back at the end where we had begun, seeing a dull glaze begin to form. I began to feel a sense of satisfaction at bringing a low pocket up to the level of the higher spots around it. I was becoming what Rachel described as "an ice nerd."

We took turns being water man and hose man, giving each other a chance to take the warmer job. The black dog watched, unmoving, black tail curled around her black nose. My neck was getting very, very stiff, from looking down constantly to make sure that I did not flood my own feet. Periodically I would stretch my head back to look at the stars and the treetops, momentarily flooding blindly while I relieved the pain. I began to realize that my body temperature was much colder than when we'd begun, and I was delighted when I saw that the hose could not reach any farther. We were almost done. My final job as hose man was to pull the hose off into the snow bank as Rachel worked the final corner, closest to the faucet.

"Turn it off, quick," she ordered, running for low ground while waggling the water stream. And something about the way she said it made me run. I disconnected the hose.

"Pull your end into the barn, quick," she barked again. Then she ran after me, met me just outside the barn door, and took the hose. She pulled the hose through a hole in a board mounted above the height of her head, then began looping it on the wooden frame next to the stove. It took whole body movements for her to urge it through the hole even a few feet. I was instructed to pull from outside the barn door, to make it easier for her, but to holler before the hose end came inside. I didn't, and Rachel unravelled a bit of the hose and took it back out the door. At that moment Jack came out of the back room, lifted the hose high above his own head, from the hole in the board, and walked his way out the door to the end of the hose, where a gallon of water sloshed out near the door slab. Before coiling the rest of the hose on the rack, he blew it out with an air compressor. I looked at the clock. Seven fifteen. It had taken us an hour and fifteen minutes to pull out the hose, flood the rink, and then return the hose, water free, to its roost.

I looked around the room. It was filled with tools. Long benches had vices, grinders, and antique cast iron drill presses. There were wrenches, saws, hammers, awls, and tools of every size and style. I couldn't begin to recognize their uses or guess at their names. Dozens of antlers were mounted on boards above the rows of windows. There were all sorts of tables. One held tools, sandpaper, and a half-built cedar box that Stella was working on. Another held toy cooking utensils and a sloppy setting of plates and saucers. An apple was balanced on each tiny toy plate. There was a foosball table, only moderately dusty. There was a wooden crate full of basketballs. Three upright freezers hummed along one long wall, flanked by an ancient-looking refrigerator. All four were labeled with three-by-five cards with a magic marker tracing of an open hand and the words, "Please close tightly."

"Look around," said Rachel. "I gotta grocery shop." And she began to rummage through the freezers one by one. The tallest shelves held plastic milk crates, each labeled with three-by-five cards held in place with loops of duct tape. She slid them in and out like drawers, hunting for just the right-sized package of each food type.

"Do you like spaghetti?" she asked.

"Uh huh." She handed me two packages of ground meat. They would turn out to be moose and caribou. The caribou was old and a bit gamey, so she would mix it with moose.

She kept extracting packages, handing some to Jack, tucking others under her arms. She gave me a cylinder of frozen orange juice, and I tucked it under an arm. The lights were all turned off, and we stood outside the barn, in the dark.

"Nice night," said Jack, staring up at the stars.

I realized that the wind had died down. I could see a glow from Traverse City on the eastern horizon. It seemed to be just enough light to allow me to follow the sound of Jack's tread ahead of me on the path. I only dropped the orange juice twice. The frozen food in my mittened hands didn't seem cold at all.

CHAPTER ELEVEN
SKATE

The house that had previously seemed too cold now felt hot. I was losing my perspective, I knew, but I felt hopeless. The zippers on both Rachel's and my snow pants were so heavily crusted with ice that they were immobile. Rachel unzipped her own boots, pulled them off, and then slid out of her snow pants. She stood them up in the sink. I was unable to bend at the knees, so she reached under my pantlegs and untied my boots, pulled them off, and matter-of-factly dropped them into the sink. I felt stupid again, already, like a toddler in a snowsuit.

"After I was about seven months pregnant with Little Jack, Tall Jack had to lace my skates for me. Don't feel bad." Rachel smiled down at me, but I did feel bad. She wasn't supposed to be more competent than me. I'd had it in my mind that she was, by nature, the lesser of the two of us. I didn't just feel bad. I felt shame.

I was able to crawl out of the snow pants on my own, but my body was stiff from the cold. She and her husband shuffled all of the clothing up to the woodstove. They moved the children's half-dried clothing onto chairs and then strategically laid out the adult clothing to melt and dry on the tile platform that supported the stove.

The cheese, bread, and fruit salad were left sitting out on the counter. In the living room, all four kids were under the covers in the king-sized bed, staring at The Weather Channel. They silently passed a jar of canned peaches back and forth between them, each one taking a sip of the juice as it passed by. I wondered if anyone in the family actually ate peaches, or if they just drank the juice. All four of them wore red flannel nightshirts with black silhouettes of moose. They appeared to be one size fits all. Even Little Jack was swimming in one. The deck of Uno cards was scattered under the bed. A heavy bound volume of the four adventures of the Borrowers lay on the bed covers. The cat chased a toy around the room, leaping, flipping it into the air.

"How was it?" asked Isabel.

"Swell. Wicked skate, come morning."

I joined them in the living room, plate loaded with fruit salad, staring at The Weather Channel. It was mesmerizing. They were all asleep within the half hour, so I found some magazines on a parson's bench and retreated into Rachel's room. The flannel sheets looked like they might have been changed just for me, so I climbed under the covers. I was freezing. I tried creating a small blanket pocket to warm my socked toes, but nothing worked. I felt as though my body temperature was plummeting, because I was no longer moving.

I was warm when I woke up. Warmer than I expected. The light was on. I was hemmed in between Little Jack, curled up in the small of my back, and Lala the dog, flush to my front, her nose exhaling directly into mine. I moved my nose and hugged the dog. It felt good. The clock radio on the dresser said two o'clock. I couldn't sleep. I flailed for a magazine, but I was pinned. There were photographs of the kids on the walls. They were home photos, but nice. There were no standard, posed school photos. The frames were all handbuilt with clear, wide wood. One picture showed the cat sitting on a pile of presents under a Christmas tree. The tree was decorated only with baby's breath and candy canes. Next to it was a six-by-ten blowup of Stella, fists full of candy canes, eyes crossed, and tufts of baby's breath protruding from both ears.

Rows of wooden pegs stood out from the wall boards, with layer upon layer of clothing. The door of a free-standing cupboard was open, and I could see the little cat asleep on top of a shelf full of shirts. The windows were beautifully shuttered on the inside, for privacy, I suppose. Shelves close to the wall beams held large Indian baskets and dance paraphernalia—a feathered fan, huge beaded and quilled headpieces, appliqued dance leggings. I would come to find out that most of them were gifts, or that Rachel had traded her own baskets for some of them.

I don't remember being drowsy enough to doze off again, but the alarm was beeping. Four thirty. It said it clearly, in searing red. Four thirty.

Some one shuffled in and banged on the top of the clock radio. I sat bolt upright in bed when it went off again. I must have dozed for a much needed fifteen minutes.

I was alone in the bed and able to get up, so I headed for the bathroom. Rachel was making coffee. I didn't care. I went straight back into the bedroom when I was finished.

I couldn't believe the rattling coming from the kitchen. She was putting away dry dishes, and the sound vibrated through the bedroom wall, because the dish shelves were on the other side. She didn't have a dishwasher. So now she had begun doing the previous night's dishes. And cooking. She was cooking. I could hear the microwave humming on and off. I dozed.

"Good morning! Skate, puppies, skate!"

"Eat shit."

"You gu-uys . . . come on."

"Eat shit."

"Eat double shit," she said, and turned on The Weather Channel.

I must have dozed again, and they must have risen. From the bedroom I could discern that breakfast was big.

"Take some asparagus, Zoey."

"It gets stuck in my braces."

"Grab those scissors and cut yourself off some little tender tips."

"Mmmm, I love hollandaise." I was beginning to recognize the sound of Stella's voice.

I pulled on a pair of pants and came out for coffee. They had all scooped some sort of leftover-looking cold cheesy casserole into bowls and had microwaved it. The asparagus with hollandaise was steaming. An open bag of tortilla chips lay on the counter. Zoey complained that she had asparagus stuck in her teeth, and Isabel pulled it out with tweezers, like a prepubescent oral surgeon. Then they were gone. It was still dark.

Rachel screamed out the door: "Build a fire!"

Rachel did dishes and packed lunches the whole time they were gone. She put the peaches from the bottom of the fruit jar into a plastic container with a snap lid and put it in Tall Jack's lunch. They were back. They were noisy. Then they were gone—all of them.

Rachel put on her boots and snapped a down vest over her hooded sweatshirt. She donned the long-cuff red plaid mittens, grabbed the garbage, and headed out the door.

I was curious, so I gulped down my coffee and dressed for the out-of-doors. I started down the path to the barns, had second thoughts, then went back inside. I grabbed the compost bucket and headed out the door again.

The morning was bright now. The ice rink was covered with skate marks. Inside, where it was quite warm, Rachel sat in a white plastic lawn chair, facing the woodstove. She was lacing up a pair of white skates with hot pink plastic guards on their blades.

"Do you want to skate?" She didn't wait for me to answer. "Far wall, back room." She pointed. "Use skate guards. Don't wreck the blades." And she was outside.

The back room was full of lumber on one end and three feet deep in sawdust on the other end. The far wall had at least two dozen sets of skates hanging on it, white, black, and buff, in every size imaginable, including two-bladed skates for babies. There were three sets of antique speed skates. Some skates had been bought new. Some had been donated. Others had been bought at garage sales. It didn't matter what size they were. They would eventually provide opportunity and entertainment for somebody.

I decided not to skate. I went outside and watched Rachel. She was well warmed up already. She was moving fast. The rink was so long that one could get up real speed. She swung an arm out to one side, like a speed skater. When she turned, she crouched down low and stretched out her thigh muscles, alternating, first one side, then the other. She zigzagged all over the entire rink, as though she didn't want to leave an inch of ice smooth without skate marks on it. She stretched out her arms and moved them in circles. It was a real workout. Periodically, she slowed and plumped into a white plastic chair next to her skate guards. She'd rest her ankles, then hop up and skate again. She threw off the vest and eventually the mittens. Finally, her sleeves were rolled up. After about twenty minutes, she slowed, did a few cool-down passes, and left the rink. She walked as comfortably in the skate guards as if she were wearing tennis shoes.

After changing into her boots, she removed the skate guards and rested them slit side down on a shelf. She wiped the snow off of the skate bases and hung them, toes down, among the children's on a special skate rack behind the woodstove. Everything was organized.

She went to the freezers and shopped again.

CHAPTER TWELVE
THE DOG STORY

"You should've skated," she said. "It was crisp." She looked out the window. "It's too mushy now. Skates would catch."

I smiled.

"Missed your window of opportunity."

That was what life was like to her, I thought, windows of opportunity. When I thought of this family, I thought of the phrase, "Play hard, work hard." She spoke often about parents who didn't know where their kids were, or didn't care. She worked them like dogs. But it was intentional. She knew where they were, what they were doing, what kind of people they were likely to become. It was hard for me to imagine the reasoning that led to the problems with administrators in the public schools that she had described. And I found myself understanding racism just a little bit better than I had before, because no one could have cared for their children better than Rachel and Jack.

She had been, for many years, the only permanent-dwelling minority parent in the school district. The things she described that had been done to her were harsh, maybe even sociopathic. "Trash," she'd said. "Trash. Twice their credentials, and they assumed I was trash." I didn't want to think about it then, there, in her churchlike, wooden-beamed living room.

Frost was dripping from the eaves, outside the windows. "Just a few more days," Rachel said. "Just give me a few more days."

"Of what?"

"Ice."

She looked pained, and I realized that she didn't want the skating rink to go away. She loved flooding it as much as skating on it. She loved making a huge slab of ice that was impervious to spring sunshine. While the rest of Little Rock County was looking forward to springtime, Rachel's family mourned it. They thrived on winter.

"Do you ever skate on the lakes?"

"Oh, yes. But not this year. Too mild. The cold bursts were too short. Sometimes we get a good cold snap without snow in the beginning of winter, but usually it snows. Then you can't see what's safe and what's not. Sometimes, if you've been out on clear ice, and you know the lakes, you can go out after a dry snow and shovel yourself off a rink, or skate if it's not too deep. But you can hit cracks and fall." She rubbed her elbow. "It's tempting to get up some really good speed on a lake. But they get pressure cracks, you know, all those square miles of ice. If there's snow on the ice, you can try to remember where the cracks are, but it's pretty easy to go too far, because you're having a good time.

"One year, the lakes froze nice, then it snowed, then the sun came out and it rained on top of the ice, and it froze again. It was really cool, because the snow inside the two ice layers made the lakes opaque. So you could ice fish a whole lake, just by skating from hole to hole. We did it on the littler lakes, the ones we knew would be frozen, the ones we knew where the springs and inlets were. It was safe. The kids had a blast.

"We caught a lot of blue gills and perch. Even Miz Z caught a bullhead. It was a nice day. It's a pain to clean all those little fish, and we did it in the kitchen here, instead of the barn, because everybody was cold. And Isabelly and Z were sorting out the fish guts. They made little piles of hearts, bladders, eyeballs. . . . They kept poking the hearts with toothpicks to make them pump. Those girls get A's in science. Now that they're in junior high, they have friends in their classes who are vegetarians and protest against dissecting things. But those two are great. They show everybody else how to do it.

"It's like that when you grow up with it, you know. You respect life. You see how fragile it is. You learn to respect your own. You see how a single bullet can tear through the spine and lungs of something twice as big as you, you learn to respect violence."

We were sitting in the chairs next to the stove, drinking coffee. Hers looked like a milkshake. She was twirling what looked like a dead mouse by the tail. I realized it was a cat toy. She tossed it over her shoulder onto the big oval rug in the living room.

"We have some friends who skated over on Lake Little Rock a week or so ago. But I wouldn't this year, not with the kids. I don't know that lake well enough."

"How many lakes do you think there are in a ten-mile radius of this place?" I motioned around the living room. I was unconsciously treating the woodstove like it was the center of the universe.

"Well, if you included little ones, I guess I'd say fifty."

"Fifty?"

"Glaciers."

"Glaciers?"

"Glaciers. They left all these scoops and ridges, dumped the sand, dumped the clay where the basins hold water, dumped the gravel, dumped the little rocks. . . . We've got the best gravel in the state."

I was learning things. I'd never thought much about gravel, that it might be quantified and qualified. I guess they put quarries in certain places for good reason.

"We say that we all live on Turtle Island. Makes sense. Sometimes it feels like we are completely surrounded by water. Hard to find high and dry ground to build a road sometimes. I imagine it felt like we lived on a big island to people who could only travel on foot."

At last, a story . . .

"Some years you can get a big melt and then a freeze, and then the ice is smooth and safe. But it has to be a *big* thaw, with lots of rain. Too scary. Too tricky. I don't like it. Not worth it. I'd rather have the rink, keep my family here.

"They drown. Kids drown. Last time I was near Chicago working in the schools, some kids drowned. Damned spring ice. . . . So I told those kids all the spring ice stories I could."

"Tell me one."

"Naw, Jesus, it's painful to think about kids drowning." She chewed at her thumbnail.

"Manaboozhou, he domesticated the first dog, you know."

At the mention of "dog," Lala was at her feet.

"La la la la la, la la la la . . ." she sang out the scale.

"Myiingunh, the wolf, became the first dog. He was Manaboozhou's best buddy. Gotta feed the dog."

She said something in Ojibwe, and the big dog jumped up and kissed her on the lips. Lala was a cross between an Irish Setter and an Afghan. And she was lovely. She looked like a jet black Irish Setter, only a little more lank and elegant. "She's a real study in domestication," Rachel would sometimes say, when the dog "invaded" her "personal space."

"Pu-uppy Chow!" Rachel called out, and Lala danced.

Rachel ran into the living room, scooped up Little Jack's used underwear and a T-shirt from the floor in front of a big cedar dresser, went down to the mudroom, tossed the laundry into the machine, and scooped out the dog food. Half regular, half lite. "We want you to live forever, Baby," she would say to the dog. She turned and grabbed three pieces of firewood before coming up the steps again. She swung open the stove door, threw them in one by one, then crimped it shut with the tool again.

"You know, you could do this, if you wanted—if you felt cold. You've gotta fend for yourself."

"How old is the dog?"

"Seven."

She adjusted the velcro straps on her sneakers. They had wide toes, like little kids' shoes. This pair was stained and dingy from everyday use. I had noticed four more identical clean, white pairs on the floor of her closet. They were balanced on top of a pile of folded Hudson's Bay woolen blankets. I had once read about an Indian chief on the northwest coast who had actually insulated his home with Hudson's Bay blankets. I was glad I hadn't said anything out loud. I knew Rachel hated the word "chief."

"So Myiingunh hung around Manaboozhou's fire to keep warm. And Manabooozhou threw him scraps of food. And Myiingunh the wolf, now First Dog, learned how to beg. It's not a very dignified skill." The dog was at her feet again, and she nuzzled her rubber sneaker toes under the animal.

"Myiingunh, in turn, helped out Manaboozhou. He helped cull out the weaker animals from the crowd—old farts like you and me. . . . (She could always personalize a story.) And Manaboozhou didn't even have to sit still very long to get a good shot. You know, this isn't even my own story. It belongs to Basil Johnston. That part of it. It belongs to him. He published it first."

"Did you ever hear it as a child?"

"Oh, yeah. But Basil made it so concise. Those words, those pretty much sound like him. I can't help myself. He made it so concise. You know, those old guys would just talk forever, just going in circles and changing the subject all the time. It's not like they just stopped what they were doing and just told stories. They were always cleaning meat or something. And it took 'em forever to get to the point."

"I could imagine."

And then she was up. "Help me make your bed."

Shame. Shame again. I should have done it.

When all the layers of blankets were in place on the queen-sized bed, she shook the red flannel moose sheet over the top. "It's a bedsheet, really," she said, "but it's easier to wash the dog fur off of it than to wash a heavy blanket. It's pretty, too." It matched the four red flannel nightshirts that Stella had brought into the bedroom and hung on pegs this morning.

I had determined to follow Rachel around, to help her through her day, to really experience her life with her. I wanted to know what it was like to be an Indian in northern Michigan. So, I followed her out to the kitchen, and I helped her, when she grabbed armsful of canning jars and carried them in to the bed.

There were several Ball canning jar and copier paper boxes stacked up between a dresser and a wooden trunk. The trunk was open and full of wool socks. She hefted the rattling jar boxes onto the bed and began sorting jars. We put them into boxes categorized by size and mouth width. I was amazed by the variety of jars. There were widemouthed half pints. They were squat. "The lids are more expensive, but they really stack nice," Rachel pointed out. Some of the half pints were roundish, short, and pretty. "For giveaways, like Christmas presents," she explained. There were tall, narrow one-and-a-half pint jars. "For when you don't quite have a quart left of whatever you are canning. They fit great on the shelves, too." She taught me how to recognize the mayonnaise jars and to put them in their own paper box, with rolled-up newspaper stuck between the rows to take up the empty space. "For juice and pickles only," she said. "You'd rather not pressure can with those. Their code does not require them to stand up to as high a pressure as something marketed as an actual canning jar." She made everything look like an art form.

Shame. There it was again, shame. I'd thought that only ignorant, back-woods, poor people canned. I mean, it was OK for my grandmother or somebody to make a batch of jam for gifts, because she was old, and she was good at it. She'd lived through the Depression. But what kind of Depression had Rachel lived through? Why was she so obsessed with canning and food?

"So maybe that part of the story, it really should belong to Basil." I re-membered Basil Johnston was an Ojibwe author she liked. She'd told me about his story, "Moose Smart, Indian Smart," at least twice.

"Maybe Basil just said it the way it needed to be said," I tried to com-fort her.

"Well, yeah! That's why I'm giving him credit for it. He's really good, you know."

Ah, so she wasn't talking about copyrights. She was enamored of his work.

"And?"

"And they were so good at hunting that they had to bury the extra meat in a cache. That's spelled c-a-c-h-e—cache." I'd forgotten that she used to be a teacher.

"Is that part Basil?"

"Uncle Bill."

"Mm-hmm." It was beginning to make sense.

"Do you know *why* they buried it in a cache?"

"To hide it from other people?"

"That's a nice answer. Why else?"

"To keep it from other animals?"

"Good answer. What about the temperature in the ground?"

"What?"

"Isn't the soil a little cooler down there, where the sun doesn't reach? Where it's moist?"

"I suppose so. People used to have root cellars."

"Good for you!"

This was definitely one of the stories she told schoolchildren. I was definitely one of her students right now. She had gone on autopilot. She pulled toward her the jar box I had filled and flipped over each of the jars so that its top was facing downward. "Keeps out dust and critters," she said. The full boxes were stacked next to the mudroom steps. The partially filled boxes were left on the bed with a few loose canning jars.

Rachel grabbed a down vest from a mudroom peg, zipped it up, and headed out the door with a full box. I put on a pair of boots and a jacket, grabbed a box, and followed her. The snow path was compact now, from many trips by many feet. The snow was soft, partially melted, and compressing under my feet. Rachel was nowhere in sight when I arrived at the barn. I pulled up a chair and waited. I instinctively sat near the woodstove, even though it was not going. I wished I could just turn it on, like a switch.

After a while, I heard crunching on the snow. I stood up, so I could see out the windows above the workbench. Rachel was coming from the house with another box. I went outside with my box of jars. She smiled, and I followed her past the next barn, then the next, and finally to an old, long, low wooden building. A pathway had been plowed between the barns, and the doorway had been dug out only recently. The battered, gray wooden door barely hung together. It was propped open with a block of wood. It was one of several doors along the side of the building.

"We leave it open ten months out of the year. We dry wood here."

And so they did. I had never seen so much lumber in my life. The boards were thick, wide, and evenly spaced, from floor to ceiling. There were narrow pathways between the stacks, crowding in at the ceiling posts. The ceiling was corrugated metal with wooden beams. There were round holes with fans spaced along the doorless back wall. She disappeared into dim light, stepping over concrete lips in the floor, moving away from the open door. I followed. Inside the next room was a series of wall posts that supported vertical layers of unused roofing metal. The sheets were twenty feet long and held in place by fifty-five-gallon steel drums.

Rachel disappeared behind the ends of the metal sheets and the other suspended farm paraphernalia that created a sort of wall. I followed. There, a thirty-foot-long shelf ran the length of the room. It was about waist high. Most of it was filled to ceiling height with boxes. Most of them were canning jar boxes. Others were copier paper boxes with labels made out of three-by-five cards: "wide mouth quarts," "small mouth quarts," "wide mouth 12 oz.," "reg. 12 oz.," "pints," "wide pints," "wide mouth half pints," "reg. half pints," "fancy half pints," "juice only," and so on. At the far end of the shelf was a very large box, and its label simply said, "boxes."

It was odd. I'd felt sorry for her, because of the small size of her house. I had thought that only poor people didn't have basements. I didn't realize that her living space included these huge unheated areas. It made sense. All the jars and boxes did were sit empty.

"Full ones, this end." She moved several boxes off of the shelf, put mine in place, then put the smaller ones on top.

"Why don't you just put all of one size in one place along the wall?" I asked.

"It's hard to safely lift something heavy over your head. It's glass. You'd have a dangerous mess here, the size of Mount Rushmore, if you dropped a box. We'd never get the glass slivers out of here, and everybody would have to wear shoes in this barn then. We've already got a barn you've got to wear shoes in. That's the pesticide barn."

I looked at the dog at her feet. "What about the dog?"

"Oh, well, pets . . . You create invisible lines that they can't cross. Lala knows she's not allowed to cross the line on the concrete in front of that barn. She'll just lie there watching us, even if we're in there for hours. She knows she's not allowed in."

"How do you teach her that?"

"Voice."

"Voice?"

"Voice. Nice voice, mean voice. It's for her own good."

"And the cat?"

"Same thing."

"Uh-huh."

She handed me two empty boxes, and we walked back to the house. It took two more trips to get all the full boxes into the old barn. Then we put the rest of the loose jars into their appropriate boxes and stacked and balanced them against the bedroom wall.

"Is there more to the dog story?" I asked.

She bent down, picked up a towel from the clean laundry heap on the kitchen floor, and began folding.

"It's not a dog story." She went into the bathroom, shut the door, and turned on the shower.

CHAPTER THIRTEEN
CRISPY FISH

She started rummaging in the refrigerator. She pulled out an open half pint of pickled jalapeños. Then she pulled out a quart of jalapeños and dumped the contents of the little jar into the big one. She ran some dishwater and washed the small jar, leaving our coffee cups to soak. She popped open a plastic container full of leftover smelt and put them on a cookie sheet and turned on the oven. While the fish heated up, she went through the shelves until she found relish. Then she made up her own batch of tartar sauce, using fresh onion. She used dill from a huge plant that hung dry in the mudroom. The mixture was spatula-ed into the clean jalapeño jar.

She chopped up a lime, then looked at the clock.

"Bus."

"Bus?"

"Bus. Gotta be there for it. Gotta be right there, where they can see me. There's got to be somebody to meet a kindergartener. Give 'em five minutes either way, before or after the time they're supposed to come. Can't not be there. They'd use it against me. These kids, they can't afford to screw up, not like the white kids. Not my kids. I complained once, when they hurt Stella. They told me I'd be punished for it. And they've really hurt my kids. . . . Shit! I can't stand here talking to you. I've got to get out there. There's no leeway. . . ."

She headed out the door with outgoing mail in her hand and carried it to the end of the driveway. I watched out the bedroom window, where I had a clean shot down the driveway. She was looking, with her head cocked. I half expected her to put her ear to the ground, like she was listening for buffalo.

The driveway was lined with wooden, roofed structures full of firewood. She began bringing in firewood, keeping an eye out for the bus, looking down at her watch. She'd leave the outside door of the mudroom cracked, then kick it open with her foot when she arrived with several pounds of split and dried firewood. Then she'd swing the door shut with her elbow and stack it, one piece at a time, in the mudroom woodbin. After about six trips, the bus showed up. Little Jack ran down the driveway, his giant red backpack waggling back and forth. I could see that they lived for one another's touch.

"Hey Mom!"

"Hey what?" She was putting smelt on a plate and pouring orange juice.

"The teacher asked us if we had breakfast today."

"I used to ask my students that, too. It was to try to pressure them into eating in the morning. I used to let the ones who had eaten get in line first. Most of the time, fifth graders didn't have it together to lie about that, until they were almost sixth graders."

"I didn't have to lie about it."

"I know."

"Guess what?"

"Chicken butt."

"She asked us *what* we ate for breakfast."

"What did you tell her?"

"Cheerios."

"Good boy."

"Try some tartar sauce, just a tiny, tiny bit on your finger. It's good to try new things."

"Yuck."

"No big deal."

Rachel and I stood at the kitchen sink and dipped the smelt into the jar of tartar sauce. The smelt were pretty dried out. This was probably the second time they were reheated.

"Mmmm . . . mmm . . . I love it when they're like this. They're like potato chips."

I supposed she was right. She popped the top off a pint of wild cranberry juice. Snap! The church key went back to her waist. She offered it to me. It was so different from what I had expected. It wasn't as tart. It had an almost rich, waxy taste to it.

Little Jack complained about the smelt, but he kept coming back for more.

"These smelt are chewy."

"Keep chewing. It's good exercise for your teeth."

Rachel sucked her piece of lime in between bites of the fish. I tried it too. She was right; they were like potato chips, especially the tails. The tails melted in my mouth. I could see how fried minnows might be pretty good.

CHAPTER FOURTEEN
THE FINE ART OF TRASH

R achel didn't have a wastebasket. She used paper bags, dog food sacks, and other sacks. She trotted them off to the barn daily. Only burnables went into the bags. Rachel had once instructed Zoey to rinse out her plastic yogurt container and put it in the recycling.

"But won't it burn?" Zoey had asked.

"Sure, but environmentally, it's better to recycle it, Z."

They didn't have trash pickup. Everything was either burned, recycled, or composted. Rachel was pleased that recycling had advanced to the point that she could mix metals, glass, and plastic. She recycled everything, even twistie ties off the bread bags. She had a plastic milk crate for recycling stationed at the foot of the mudroom steps, so that she could toss into it from the kitchen. After it got fairly full, the canning lids, yogurt lids, and other things she tossed began to bounce out. A couple of times a day, as she passed by doing other things, she would pick up the items that had missed the crate and rearrange the crate's contents to reduce the bounce. Several full crates were stacked by the base of the woodpile, next to a twelve-foot folding ladder ("For changing light bulbs") and some massive, prehistoric stone implements.

Rachel had made several passes around the house picking up stray bits of children's paper. Then she sorted through the magazines on the parson's bench. Finally, she headed out the door again, shopping bag full of garbage under one arm, compost under the other.

"Is there anything else to go to the barn?" I asked.

"Just your sorry ass." She'd figured out that I was following her around, and she was shaking her head. "You could read a book or something while I'm doing this."

But I didn't. I followed. The path to the barns wound around a huge bush in the yard. It was at least twenty feet tall.

"What is that?"

"Wild hazelnut."

"It's so tall. How do you pick them?"

"How do you know if I pick them or not?"

But I knew. I knew she wouldn't waste a single nut, and she'd manage to turn the whole experience into some sort of lifetime experience for her children.

"How do you pick them?"

"See how skinny the trunks are? It's not just one hazelnut bush any more. It's a bunch of them. One of us just climbs into the middle and bends the trunks down to the ground. Then somebody else picks them."

"Do you get a lot?"

"No. I think all I've got here is female. Just a few nuts is all I get. Some years are better than others. Maybe we get a few pounds."

"Are they like the commercial nuts?"

"Same taste. Same size nut. The commercial ones have a shell twice as big, though, but it's all air."

I stared into the thick bush. I couldn't imagine climbing in between the scratchy branches. There were little round, brown things on top of the snow in between the narrow trunks.

"Are those hazelnuts that have just fallen?"

"What? No, those are rabbit turds."

"Oh."

"Sex."

"What?"

"Sex. They're having sex now."

"Oh."

"Right there. In the hazelnut bush."

"Why?"

"Why sex?"

"Why there?"

"Whew! You had me worried. Pretty hard for a hawk or an owl to get at them there, because the hazelnut branches are so stiff right now. The grouse hang out there a lot, too. They like to eat the buds sometimes.

"See how it's all beaten down below the level of the rest of the snow? See how they've got tunnels? It's like a little bunny singles' bar in there. You should see when the babies are hopping all over the yard here, especially under the satellite dish, in the poison ivy there. There are tulips there, and they all look like Easter Bunnies."

"Does all that rabbit poop get stinky?"

"Are you joking?"

"No."

"There's not enough of it. Besides, it's good for the tree."

"I thought it was a bush."

"It's also a tree."

"Uh huh."

"Really. Look at the size of that dog. Like you don't think that maybe I've got a bigger problem with dog poop? I mean, look at her. She's got separation anxiety. Do you think she goes very far to poo?"

I looked around the yard. There were piles of dog poo along the path.

"Remind me to get a shovel, when we get to the barn. Ah well, could be worse."

"What do you mean?"

"Well, the hazelnut bush could be a singles' bar for skunks."

"When do skunks breed?"

"Don't worry. You missed it. Two weeks ago."

"Here?"

"Naw . . . under the satellite dish."

I'll never know if she was kidding.

Taking the garbage to the barn was more complicated than I thought. She crumpled up some old magazines and newspapers and made a bed of them in the dingy old parlor stove that heated the workshop. Then she tore the garbage bag open sideways and laid it down. After that, she went into the back room, scooped up a half bucketful of wood shavings, and scooped them into the stove by hand. The door wasn't big enough to toss in the whole half bucketful. Then she fetched a heavy-duty metal dustpan and swept up the sawdust and ashes that spilled.

She took the five-gallon bucket over to the freezers and began to "shop." The doors of the freezers were filled with cylinders of frozen juice. The kids didn't get many soft drinks, but I didn't imagine that they minded. I thought of the role orange juice played in my own childhood. Even now, I considered it a treat. Rachel took a half dozen cylinders from the top shelf, then shifted all the other cylinders up a shelf, until the bottom shelf was empty. I was beginning to understand her, and I automatically understood that the newest juice would go on the bottom.

"What's in the fridge?" I asked.

"Look for yourself. No sense in taking my word for everything. I could be lying like a rug."

Apples.

I peered in the third freezer, the one to the farthest right. I had never seen her open it. It contained nothing but frozen gallon jugs of apple cider.

"Hey, hey, HEY!" Rachel scolded. She pointed with a sneakered toe to a three-by-five card at the bottom corner of the freezer door. I obeyed the sign. I bent down and pushed the corner of the door shut tightly.

CHAPTER FIFTEEN
COMPOST

Rachel took a running start and skidded across the ice rink with the full compost bucket. She dumped the slop, then called me to her. I obeyed. For some reason, I chose to go across the rink, rather than around it. It wasn't as flat as it had looked the night before. The gently mounded high spots were what she called "volcanoes." On warm days, water ran under the surface of the slab, collected in low spots, then emerged through weak spots in the ice. "It's sort of like a spring," she said. "Water runs through cracks and crevices in the earth, and then it gets to something it can't go through, so it goes up. Up is the easiest way in those spots, I guess. You can skate on the mounds just fine. You glide right over them." There were places that looked bubbly, too. But when I walked over them, the ice on the top was thick and strong.

"Looky here."

She was pointing at the compost heap. It was revolting, mostly onion ends, apple cores, and coffee grounds. It smelled awful. I'd had no idea the stuff was rotting like that, right under our noses in the kitchen.

"Jeez. Get your nose out of the compost. What are you, crazy?"

"I don't get it."

"Footprints. Tiny ones, see?"

Rachel's compost had been keeping the local bunnies beefed up for their sexual escapades, I guessed. They'd been grazing on the less revolting parts of the compost heap that emerged from the snow. There were a lot of littler footprints, too, I saw—sweet, tiny, perfect footprints that had been made when the snow was soft from the sunshine—maybe even right before we got there.

"Did you see this one?"

A tiny set of footprints trailed away from the others, obviously pointed away from the food pile. Then the trail vanished into thin air.

"Mouse?"

"Used to be."

"What is it now?"

"Dinner."

"What?"

"See the wings? See? See here, the front part of the wings, below the elbow, touched down here, just before it grabbed the little thing. Then the tail hit, just before it took off."

"That's horrible."

"No, no, it's beautiful, in its own way. You've got to look at it like that. Mice reproduce faster and easier than owls. That's what they do. They hunt."

"In broad daylight?"

"Sure. Lots of times. Haven't you ever seen an owl out in the daytime?"

"I've never seen an owl."

"But you've seen lots of mice."

"A few."

"In cages?"

"I don't have them in my house."

"Neither do I. Got 'em in the barns and the orchards though. Farmers like skunks. We just love having skunks in the orchards. Coyotes and foxes, too. They eat mice.

"There are lots of different ways to farm, you know. You can farm chemical intensive, which is usually the corporate way, and then you can farm labor intensive. A cherry farmer mows the rows and cold air drainage fields regularly to keep down the mice. When the grass is short, the hawks are much more efficient."

"Do mice eat the cherries?"

"No, they eat the young trees. They chew the bark off, especially in a bad winter. Some years you can see where the snow line was during a particularly warm spell the winter before, because the mice chew up all the little trees and bushes as high as they can reach. They can't reach very high, obviously, so it's just a band of a few inches. It's very recognizable."

"Do you use mousetraps?"

"Are you joking? There are thousands and thousands of mice out there. It probably takes pounds and pounds of 'em just to keep a coyote fed for a day. We poison them, just like everybody else. Some farmers just use more poison, that's all. Maybe they've got too much acreage to keep mowed by themselves, or they're sick with the flu. I mean, farming is farming. If you think vegetarians don't impact other living things, or wildlife in particular, think again. Does this look *wild* to you?" She gestured around at the straight rows of cherry trees that disappeared into the distance in every direction, on both sides of the road.

"A little bit," I confessed.

"Not even close. But you can still make it a pretty good place for critters. They have to be managed, though. Their habitat is being chopped up and isolated pretty badly around here. We're starting to have bear problems."

"Bear problems?" Maybe there was a story in it. . . .

"Yeah. People are moving into their habitat. People say, 'Ooh, there's a big, bad bear in my backyard.' And I say, 'Eeeyuu . . . there are a bunch of inconsiderate suburbanites in that poor bear's backyard.' I mean, they want to live in the country, what do they expect? Country on *their* terms?"

She skidded a plastic lawn chair onto the ice, gave it a glide, then sat in it where it stopped. She threw her face up to the sun, unzipped her jacket, and stretched out her feet. She looked settled in, so I grabbed a lawn chair and sat beside her.

"Why are the chairs white?"

"They came from the store that way."

I laughed. I'd thought that it was for some esoteric reason, like blending in with the winter landscape. From listening to the kids, I'd learned that they took turns pushing each other around on the ice in the chairs when they skated.

"Cache. C-a-c-h-e."

"OK."

"So the meat was cool, and it was supposed to keep. But Manaboozhou and Myiingunh were going farther and farther away to hunt game. They were so successful that they had caches just about everywhere, and they were forgetting where the oldest ones were."

The dog story . . .

"And sometimes they'd come to a cache and Manaboozhou would say, 'Whooh, Myiingunh, this meat is getting pretty rank. Fu-unky!' Because they were killing more than they could eat, and that's not the way it's supposed to be done, is it?"

She was looking at me over the top of her sunglasses and shaking her head in a negative motion, prompting me.

"No, I guess not."

"Uh uh. They were being greedy. And there are these guys out there who have a very important job to do. They fight greed. This is very important. Can you imagine what the world would be like if nobody said no to greed?"

"But Manaboozhou and the dog weren't really being greedy on purpose, were they?"

"Does it matter? If it messes up the balance of things, does it matter? After all, it's not their job to fight greed in this particular story—it's their job to be greedy. It's just a story. They're greedy. On purpose or not, they are committing a serious faux pas."

"Of course."

"These monsters are called the *michikiniibigag*."

"Monsters?"

"Yeah, monsters."

"I thought you said there were no bad spirits."

"Monsters. In English, it used to mean an animal that is made up from the parts of more than one animal. I was sort of hoping it still meant that. I mean, doesn't it? I'm gonna have to look it up, now. You've got me worried.

"So they're monsters. Snakes. Snake bodies. Snake skin. Snake eyes. Snake lips. Antlers."

"Antlers."

"Mmm hmm . . . Little dried-stick-looking antlers some of them, big goofy moose antlers some of them. Monsters. But nice guys. They've got a job to do. That's the gift the creator gave them—their job. Because, face it, the antlers weren't much of a gift. They were a real liability for a snake, if you think about it."

"I see."

"No, you don't. You're just humoring me. You've got to live it to believe it."

"I believe you."

"No you don't! If you believed me, you'd be as crazy as I am. I constantly drift in and out of these stories, back and forth, between doing the laundry, driving the car, and kissing really big fish on the lips. I am a product of my environment. It's not just an Indian versus non-Indian thing, I think. It's urban versus rural, too. There are urban Indians, too. I know a lot of them. We're allowed to live anywhere we want now. Took a little bloodshed to get us there. We've got to buy back the real estate first, of course, but . . . never mind."

"So these antler things—"

"Please, they're not *things*. They have human personality traits, just like you and me."

"OK."

"So they fight greed. And they had this really big meeting, and they decided that this really good team had to be broken up."

"Team?"

"Manaboozhou and First Dog."

"OK."

"And . . . it was springtime, like now."

"Was it really, or are you just saying that?"

"Really. Why do you think I'm telling this story?"

"I'm not sure. But keep going."

"School bus."

"What?"

"School bus. It just went by on the road."

I heard the bus wheels squeak at the end of the driveway by the house. Little Jack had somehow appeared during the conversation and had been sitting on Rachel's lap. He jumped up, shuffled across the ice, and went down the path. He disappeared around a curve. You couldn't even see the house from here, but I could hear the dog barking. Jack was yelling, but he was too far away to understand.

Rachel got up, went to the pump, and rinsed out the compost bucket. She picked up the frozen juice from the snowbank in front of the barn door and put it in the bucket. She disappeared around the bend in the pathway, too. It was very quiet, very peaceful. I needed a break from them all.

CHAPTER SIXTEEN
COMMUNITY PROPERTY

Rachel was warming up a Tercel. She opened up her door. ("Windows freeze up here, it's an awfully moist place. . . . Don't force it, you can break the mechanism." She and Tall Jack were the king and queen of careful, preventive equipment use. They squeezed machinery dry.)

"Do you want to come?"

I wasn't sure. But she wasn't volunteering information, so I hopped in on the passenger side. The door squeaked when I opened it.

"Remind me—silicone spray, when we get back."

I hadn't even remembered the shovel.

"What are we doing now?"

"I have to go check on Isabel."

"She didn't get off of the bus?"

"No. She's running interference for Z. She wasn't supposed to go back yet, but she doesn't like it here with me, because I say no sometimes."

"Why is she with you?"

"They ask me to sometimes. Just tell me flat out, they can't handle her anymore. Things are going on that I don't know about. Izzy tells me sometimes. She says it gets pretty violent. It's not my place to say. But Izzy says that it gets pretty violent against Z. I don't ask. The Divine Miz doesn't tell me.

"I think, most of the time, they just buy her off, leave her with her computer, CD player—never say no. It takes a lot of work to say no to kids. At our house, it gets pretty ugly sometimes. I once grounded Stella for two whole months. She behaved well for years after that. Don't remember what I grounded her for.

"Miz Z goes on all of our trips with us. They just pull her out and do the paperwork for homeschooling, and off to the bush she goes with us. And then, sometimes, in her real life, she's off to Washington, D.C., or Los Angeles, or someplace exciting. The girls are incredibly jealous. I won't even take them to Disneyland."

No, I didn't imagine she would.

"I'd drive hundreds of miles to take them to pick wild blueberries though."

I imagined she would.

"So, did I tell you about the snakes with antlers?"

"Yes, you did."

"OK, so they had a big meeting."

"And decided to break up the team."

"Yes, they were just too efficient at hunting, Manaboozhou and First Dog. And they didn't have it together to think about things like waste and overharvesting yet. They had to learn the hard way.

"So the Michikiniibigag lured Myiingunh out onto thin ice on the river. It was springtime, like now, sunny, like this."

"How did they lure him?"

"I haven't thought that part up yet."

"You mean you're making this up as you go along?"

"No! I told you, it's not just *my* story. It's everybody's story. Sometimes, we start to tell stories, and then we find out that somebody else has another part to the story, either before or after the part that you've got. This is human history. It goes on forever. No one person can memorize the whole thing. So each of us gets a little piece of it, and, if we're lucky, we get to hear three, four, six different sections, all tied together, in just one lifetime. That's why they call us a *culture*, and not just a bunch of individuals. That's why it's sort of like a whole library burns down when an old person dies. Eddie told me that."

"Eddie told you what?"

"That it's like a whole library burns down when an old person dies. Do you know why?"

"Why?" I felt like the story was about to take a wild turn.

"Because maybe only one person still alive has the piece to one of the stories, and then there would be a big gap, and one of Manaboozhou's descendants would go out and do something stupid, because there wasn't a bad example for him not to follow."

"Didn't Eddie tell you any other cultural reasons for mourning the loss of an old person?"

"He didn't give me *any* reasons. I'm just filling in on my own."

"Oh."

"I know there are other reasons. I'm not stupid. We're human beings, not Hollywood stereotypes."

"I didn't mean anything. I'm sorry."

"No, I'm sorry. I know you didn't. I was off in storytelling mode."

We were back next to the big house with the turret. The Lexus was there, and two Volvos. Four chows barked and jumped up at Rachel's car.

"You can come in, if you want."

The house was cathedral-like, in beiges and whites. The sofas matched. The windows stretched up to the second floor. The stairs were carpeted. There was a lot of wood trim, and, before I'd seen Jack's handiwork, I would have thought it was an extravagant use of wood as decoration. There were large potted plants all over, and the painting over the fireplace looked like Woodland Indian art.

The woman who was introduced to me as Zoey's mother was at least six feet tall. She was warm and gracious. She was obviously upper middle class. Rachel was very comfortable with her, and with all of the other people we were introduced to. I hadn't expected this. I hadn't expected Rachel to be able to float into a room like that. She'd described the racism in Little Rock County so strongly, that I didn't think she could do that. But she did. In her paint-stained blue jeans and hooded sweatshirt, she charmed those people.

No, no, the girls were fine, we were told. They could stay the night and get on the bus together in the morning. They were upstairs, on the Internet.

"Isabel, come say hello to your mother," the woman sang out. Izzy peeked down, waved, and disappeared. Rachel blew her a kiss.

"Would either of you care for a glass of wine?"

"Not today," said Rachel. And we left.

I'd wished she'd said yes. I wanted to see who these people were. I wanted to know how they related to someone like Rachel. They were the gentry, I thought, and she was not.

75

We were barely out of the driveway before she picked up the story. This was unusual for her.

"So they lured him out onto the ice. I don't know how. I've never heard that part of the story yet. I couldn't even begin to tell you whether or not there are people alive who have that part of the story. So, now that you've pointed out the gap, I'll spend the rest of my life looking for it. Either I'll hear it from somebody, or I'll live it, figure it out, and throw it in.

"So, anyhow, the part of the story that I started out with was Basil's. But he didn't publish the whole story. Maybe he didn't know it. Maybe he didn't feel like it. It's not like we tell you guys everything. You'd package it up and sell it, if we did. You wouldn't need us any more. You'd figure you knew more about our stories than we do."

"So which part of the story was from your Uncle Bill, and which part was from you?"

"I don't remember any more. It's not like I go around memorizing these stories. We *live* them. They only have meaning to us because we live them. They are very practical stories, really. They teach stuff."

"OK."

"So they lured him out on this thin ice.

"Now, this is the part where you turn to those kids, and you say, 'What happens when something that weighs about as much as you do—oh, a hundred-pound dog, say—goes out on thin ice in the springtime, with water running under it?'

"And the kids say, 'Ice breaks?' And you say, 'Exactly.'

"Because you want them to think about it in their own personal terms, maybe even think about their dogs, too. Some people do really dumb things with their dogs. If your dog falls in, it's too slippery for it to get out, and you can't get it out, either. That's why they say to take big spike nails in your pocket, when you go ice fishing. So if you fall in, you can stick them in the ice and use them to pull yourself out."

We were barely crawling along on the dirt road. She turned to me and asked, "Now, even if you're a good swimmer, can you swim in freezing cold weather?"

She was shaking her head no, so I answered, "No."

"That's right. Hypothermia kills in just about fifteen minutes. But don't count on a full fifteen minutes for someone to show up and pull you out. You'll stiffen up way before then."

This was gruesome.

"It was several days before Manaboozhou found his best buddy's cold, stiff body downstream along the river."

"That's horrible."

"But Manaboozhou spoke to the spirits. He told them, 'Don't take it out on the dog. My dog does whatever I teach it to do. I am the one who is half human, and I am the one who should take responsibility. Don't blame the dog.'

"So the spirits allowed Manaboozhou to breathe the breath of life back into First Dog. But, ever since that time, dogs don't live as long as people. . . . It's because Manaboozhou screwed up, and we all have to live with the consequences of his actions. But we don't hate Manaboozhou for it. We would never throw him away, just because he messed up. We're all going to mess up, all of our lives.

"But, because our pets don't live as long as we do, we have an obligation to make every day they spend on this planet a good one. We have to take care of them, get their shots, take them to the vet. If it's really cold, we have to make sure that they have shelter. In the summertime, when it's hot what do we really, really have to make sure that they have plenty of?"

"Water?"

"That's right, water. They'll die without it. And what else do they absolutely live for?"

"I give up."

"Our attention."

Lucky Lala, I thought. She spent most of her day touching one of the family, or curled up in one of many spots that belonged specifically to her. During meal preparation, she spent most of her time on her back, between the kitchen and the living room. Everyone that crossed over her said, "Pay the toll before you cross the bridge." Her tummy was scratched every time.

Rachel looked over in my direction, after backing the car up next to the house door and turning off the engine. "You said you wanted a thin ice story."

The house smelled like spaghetti sauce. Little Jack was watching The Weather Channel. Stella was lying on the bed, watching the television upside down. "How was it?" she asked her mother. She took a bite out of her apple, and I couldn't help but get involved with the way her teeth looked upside down, just like I was a kid at a slumber party.

"OK."

"Why didn't you just phone?" It suddenly dawned on me.

"They never take it off of the machine. Wouldn't have done any good."

About nine o'clock that night, the Lexus showed up in the driveway, long after everyone but me was asleep. I watched from the bedroom window as Isabel and Zoey climbed out, bookbags in hand. The driver of the Lexus tried to make a three-point turn in the driveway, but seemed to be trapped on a basin of ice. I pulled on shoes and a jacket and pushed. The power window opened on the driver's side, and a strange hand waved in thanks, as the car pulled out into the darkness.

By the time I was back inside, Izzy and Z were under the covers in the queen-sized bed in Rachel's room, where I had been reading. So I decided to shower. When I got out of the shower, Lala was there on the bathmat again, wearing a fluorescent pink wig and a pair of sunglasses with lenses the shape of the state of Texas. I curled up in a bunk bed in the little cedar bedroom off the mudroom.

In a little while, Zoey thumped out of the bedroom. "You guys, my mom sent twenty dollars for groceries. You guys?"

CHAPTER SEVENTEEN
FREEZING RAIN

One morning there was a freezing rain. Before leaving for the barns at his usual ungodly hour, in the dark, Tall Jack called his instructions into the door of the house: "Listen to the radio for the school report." It wasn't on for another hour yet, but there would be a two-hour school delay, due to the ice. Rachel was elated, and she'd resolved to coerce her children into a final skate. We went with them, after the sun came up.

The path to the barns was too icy to walk on, and everyone walked in the snow on the side. Every step was measured. We had to wait a second for each footfall to sink in, because the ice crust was so thick. The hardest part was walking across the plowed barnyard, when we ran out of snowy stretch.

Rachel had her skates on first. Little Jack didn't want to skate. I suspected that none of them did, but they were humoring her. She put on her pink plastic skate guards and took her chair out the door with her. I stood in the doorway and watched her. She humped over, using the chair like a walker, slipping and lurching. Then she sat down in the chair to take off the skate guards. "Get two bucketsful of wood shavings from the back room, and use them to make a path to the rink for the kids. Don't be stingy. Use more if you need to." Then she continued her hobble to the rink. I helped Zoey with her skate laces. Her fingers seemed too long to maneuver around the grommets. Her skates were the molded plastic kind that some children use, the kind with extra ankle support, but they were immense and would've fit a medium-sized man.

I don't know why, but I decided to join them. Tall Jack had built a fire in the barn, before going out to the orchard, so I didn't mind taking the boots off for a few moments. I fell twice, before I got to the rink.

The ice looked spongy in places, and there were small holes to skate around. But everyone seemed to be finding good places to skate, down on the low end of the rink. The barnyard slanted ever so slightly, and even though Tall Jack tried to level up the ground while compacting the rink each year, it never worked out quite right. The rest of the year, the spot was Rachel's garden, so it got plowed up into fluffy soil every spring.

Everyone skated slower than usual, and no one fell but Rachel. She lay on her back for a long time, winded. "Ignore her. She always does that," said Isabel. The dog went straight for her face.

We all took turns pushing Little Jack around the rink in a plastic lawn chair. It was a lot more fun than I thought it would be, because one could lean on the chair a little bit. It took some of the strain off my ankles. Everyone started to push him back and forth in the chair, as though they were playing hot potato. He never gave up the toothless grin. "Oh, quit, before he dies of happiness!" Rachel called out. Then one leg of the chair caught in a melt hole, and the chair tumbled sideways. Little Jack was all arms and legs. When he sat up, he had blood on his face, and his other front tooth was missing. He was silent, as though he was still trying to process what was happening. Then he began a slow wail.

"Jeez, Lil' Jack, where's your other tooth?" Isabel said, scratching over the surface of the ice with her mittens. Jack wailed louder. "My toof, my toof, itf all your fault, you loft my toof!" Blood dribbled down his chin.

Rachel looked at me like she was afraid I was going to call social services. "It's OK. It was really loose anyways. He just tore his gums a little is all. It'll all be good as new by the time he graduates from high school."

"What about the toof fairy, you affholes?" screamed Jack.

"It's OK," said Stella. "You can write her a note."

But eventually the tooth was located, with its telltale speck of bloody gum that kept it from blending into the ice rink. Stella was put in charge of its safety. They changed into their boots, hung up their skates, and headed back to the house. "C'mon Jack, I'll split a jar of applesauce with you," Stella said.

Rachel took a roundish pair of snowshoes down from the barn wall. They were on pegs above various tools and extension cords. "There's another pair. Still wanna follow me?" she moved her eyebrows up and down like Groucho Marx.

"Uh, sure."

So she laced me up, then laced herself up. She handed me a hockey stick, then motioned me out the door. We used the hockey sticks like walking sticks. I followed her out to a road past the barnyard. It made a sudden downward turn, and I fought to stay in place on the ice crust. It was overcast and dark. There was no hope for sun to melt the surface so I could get a grip.

We walked what seemed like at least half a mile, past huge blocks of fruit trees of various ages and sizes. She called out their varieties to me by name, but they were meaningless. They all just looked like trees. I could hear a chainsaw in the distance. She told me it was Jack, pruning trees on the other side of the farm. We turned sharply into a block of young trees that ran in long rows. The rows disappeared over the crest of a hill. She began whacking ice off the first tree.

She gave me very careful instructions and demonstrated it several times, before she let me try it with my hockey stick. "Like this—insert, then hit on a big branch—tap, tap, tap. Then pull it straight out. Then in on the other side, like this. Insert—tap, tap, tap—slide. Got it? Don't bang the buds, that's this year's blooms and fruit. Sl-i-i-i-de the stick in. First the left side, and then the right, so we don't hit each other with the sticks. Insert. Tap, tap, tap. Slide out. OK?" And then she started to work her row and left me far behind. She met me coming back on the next row, when I crested the hill and realized that I was only halfway there. I began to feel hungry. The whole family had eaten bean and meat burritos that morning, but I had abstained. Now the coffee was gurgling in my empty stomach.

"You can go back if you want, but I'd be grateful if you finished the row, first, so I know it's been done. I know it's not what you came here for."

No, hard work wasn't what I'd come for. I'd come to pick her brain, and I'd thought it would be easy. I had confused *self*-employed with *un*-employed. I had envisioned myself sitting by a roaring fire, sipping wild mint tea, and talking for hours on end, until I was stiff from sitting. I hadn't imagined anything like this.

So I stayed. It took a couple of hours until we finished. Rachel easily did twice as much as me.

"It's just like anything else," she would say. "You develop a rhythm and your own way of doing it."

I couldn't talk. I was out of breath. We walked back to the barns silently. She hung up the snowshoes, propped the hockey sticks against a bench by the door, and rummaged in the freezers. She still had the presence of mind to plan another meal.

"Grab the shovel."

I thought I would be helpful and dig out the dog mess from the pathway, but the stools were frozen in place with a heavy clear glaze.

"Leave the shovel there," she laughed. "It'll keep."

Inside the house, she sorted out the bag of food she'd brought from the freezers.

"Did anybody bring in a milk from the snowbank yesterday?"

There was a long silence.

"No."

"Shit! Well, drink powdered. It's OK. We all like powdered, except Dad, and he doesn't drink milk anyhow. Aw, c'mon, you guys, I hate when you detonate a nuclear device in the living room when I'm gone! Why aren't you in school?"

"Cancelled."

"So clean up after yourselves. We got no slaves on this plantation, except me. Make the couch, now! Zoey, you *do* live here. . . . You're *not* a guest. Move, move, MOVE!"

And they tidied up a little bit. But not much.

"My mom sent twenty dollars for groceries," said Zoey.

"You still have to work."

"I know, I'm just telling you."

"Next time we go to town, we'll buy Clue. But first, you've got to earn it. At least get it to the point where I can find the floor. Somebody put away the dry dishes, so we can wash up another sinkful. Boy, you guys are slobs!"

I guess she was tired. But she was also pretty cranky. So I washed the sinkful of dishes. The hot water felt incredibly good on my cold hands, and I could understand why Rachel said she didn't care whether or not she had a dishwasher. But my legs were tired, and I longed to sit. Rachel was scooping peanut butter and jam onto bread, making two sandwiches. I imagined she was eager to sit, too. We plopped into the chairs by the stove.

"Can we have cocoa?" asked Zoey.

"Z, can you *make* cocoa?" Rachel asked.

"No."

"Ever tried?"

"No."

"Good time to start. Green canister, shelf above the stove. Right-hand side, behind the coffee. Read the directions. Izzy, get her a measuring cup. Make ten cups, Zoe. Ten cups."

"Ten cups."

"You can do it, Zoe."

"How many cups?"

"Ten, same as the number of fingers you've got. Ten cups, Zoe. Ten cups."

"Why did we do that, out there?"

"Ice is heavy. It's heavier than just a regular rain that runs off. Tall Jack tries to prune the trees into a T-shape, so they don't split down the middle if they get heavy ice or heavy snow. But little trees, they break anyways. It's not going to melt today like I thought, so we gave the trees a little help. Thanks for the help."

"Did any of them split?"

"A few of them."

"Will they die?"

"Maybe. Maybe not. Maybe not for a year or so, if the split leaves a sore where disease gets in. The trees are at least seven years old before they produce even a little crop. They are a long-term investment. They have to be treated like little babies."

"How many cups?"

"Ten cups, Z."

"Which pot should I use?"

"Experiment, Zoe. The worst that will happen is that you'll have to wash an extra pot."

"Do I have to wash the pot, too?"

LIARS AND FAKERS

Zoey did not spill the cocoa on my shirt when she brought it to me, but she came close. Rachel quickly pulled a large, blue, wrinkled handkerchief from the front pocket of her sweatshirt. She shook it out into something less than a wad and began the wiping process, before the non-spill even occurred. I wondered if she hadn't spooked Zoey. "Don't worry, Zoe, someday you'll glide." Rachel was encouraging, but she never looked up from her cocoa at the girl. I could definitely imagine Zoey gliding down a runway.

The conjoined twins sat watching us from the wall seat. Rachel let them sip. The Divine Miz Z, unable to sit still, wandered around the living room picking up wads of black dog fur. Isabel climbed into her mother's lap.

"You are pretty like a movie star," Rachel whispered into her ear.

"Thanks, Mom. You are too."

"No, I mean really, I mean it."

I wondered how she could lie to her like that. Isabel looked like the front of a Pontiac. Rachel had tried to explain to me about Indian noses once, in one of her verbal side trips, when I was trying to get information. "There are three types of Indian noses: flat, bulb, and beak. They tend to cluster within communities. It's just like that with a small gene pool.

"One time, I got a call from somebody who said, 'I saw you in Sault Ste. Marie yesterday, but you had a moustache.' It was a cousin, a first cousin. His sister and I used to look so much alike that people got us confused. We walked alike. We moved alike. But she was two years older than me, so she filled out. And then, people mistook her little brother for me. It was my cousin, it was him, I'm sure of it."

"Did they speak?"

"No. She just said it was me that walked across the room. She saw me from the back, and I walked my walk across the room, and I sat my sat, and I moved my hands like I move my hands. And so she went over to say, 'Hi,' but I had a moustache. So she said, 'Where are you from?' And he said, 'Apisabigo.' And that's where he's from. So, you see? It was him."

"Are you sure?"

"Yes, I'm sure."

"How many people live in Apisabigo?"

"Including the suburbs?"

"Sure."

"Twenty-five to thirty-five, depending upon the weather."

"What kind of work do your parents do, Zoey?" I asked her, when Rachel called her over to drink the cocoa.

"Um, my Mom doesn't do anything, but my Dad is a basketball coach. That's why he has to travel a lot."

It was hard to contain myself. "No wonder your family is so tall, Zoey."

"Why?" said Isabel, "Does playing basketball make you tall?"

Her mother pushed her off of her lap and threw them both out of the room. Little Jack followed.

Rachel looked settled in, so I started to ask questions. I knew I wasn't going to get any more Indian stories out of her until I let her unload about racism first.

"Why didn't you want to stay for a glass of wine with those people?"

"We were crashing a dinner party."

"Oh. I thought maybe you wouldn't be comfortable with them."

"Oh, no, I can hold my own with them. I'm twice as educated as most of them. If I get into trouble, I can throw that around. But there's no need to really. You can almost always find common ground with somebody.

"The main thing I end up hating about a small-scale party like that, is that somebody eventually asks you to tell a traditional story . . . like you're an audiocassette, and all they have to do is push a button."

She was warming up.

"Yes, Massa. I be ready to shuck-n-jive for y'all. . . ." She said it like a college professor, in perfect midwestern English, adding to the absurdity of the statement. "I mean, I know they don't expect me to run into the bathroom and come out dressed like Pocahontas. . . . But, they expect me to create an illusion, to paint perfect northwoods Hiawatha stereotypes in their minds, like theater. That's a lot of work. Performers are exhausted after they do a job like that. It takes a lot of mental energy."

"So what do you do when they ask you to tell a story?"

"I tell them that most of the stories I know are about education rather than entertainment, and that they would be didactic and boring."

"And if that doesn't work?"

"Have you been following me to parties? I tell them that they're putting me on the spot, and that I don't want to."

"I guess that would work."

"It does."

"Do you go to many parties?"

"No. I'm a recluse. I live for quiet moments alone."

"Oh."

"It's OK. You don't have to leave your chair," she assured me.

"So, do you get along with those people?"

"What people?"

"Like the people at the dinner party."

"People who came here from somewhere else?"

"I guess so."

"Why wouldn't I?"

"Are they prejudiced against Indians?"

"Yeah, but they don't know it."

"What do you mean?"

"They think they like me, and they're proud of themselves for inviting me in for a glass of wine."

"Why wouldn't they?"

"Oh, because Indians are dirt."

"Why do you think they think that about you?"

"They don't directly, but they do indirectly."

"How?"

"Remember what happened to Stella at school?"

It was hard to forget. It seemed surreal. Rachel, years before, had escaped from an abusive marriage in Colorado, from a public school administrator who continued to harrass and threaten her for several years. She had been recruited by NASA to work with a group at the Air Force Academy, developing math and science educational materials to be distributed in schools throughout the country. She'd been forced to flee the area, because of continued harrassment by her former spouse.

She had given up her job, her security, her home, everything, and had arrived back home in northwest lower Michigan with tiny Stella. The ex couldn't let go, and began summoning Rachel back to Colorado through visitation issues. The judge wisely ordered a guardian ad litem for Stella, an attorney in the state of Colorado who would supervise the visitation and the child's welfare. Stella was in elementary school already and quite good at describing things that happened to her, so the father never got more than one visit.

Rachel said that the visit to the father was one of the most frightening times of her life. She really felt that he was capable of killing the child. "To hurt me," she said, "because he'd taken everything else away from me, and Stella was the only thing left to hurt me with."

It had been hard for me to understand, when Rachel described "parents' daily fear that they will outlive their offspring." I've never been married. But, after being with her family, I understood how attached they were, literally—always touching, always thinking about one another. They spent their free time entangled with one another. Even willowy Zoey was seduced into sitting close in with the family and pets. And Tall Jack and Stella seemed genuinely in love with one another as father and daughter.

Why, then, didn't the first husband care for his child? "Some people are hurt as children," said Rachel, "so they don't know how to love. They are so damaged that they cannot even bond with their own children. And they are so full of contempt for themselves that they cannot understand how anyone else could love them. So they start to hate the people around them, because they think they must be faking their love.

"They are incredible fakers, you know. They never have a moment of relaxation, never a moment of downtime. They carefully think out every utterance before it leaves their mouths. They can have incredible social skills at times. Remember the famous murderer in Milwaukee who dismembered his victims? Remember how he could talk the police into giving his victims back to him, even though they were naked, bleeding, and crying? People like that spend their lifetimes watching normal behavior, and then they figure out, through trial and error, when they need to use it. But it's a challenge for them. When they relax, they get mean. It's behavior that was pushed on them as kids. Some people can get over child abuse, but others can't. If they were really, really hurt, they could only find self-satisfaction in hurting others. It gives them the same power that their abusers had.

"It's all very weird. You don't understand why they are abusing you, when abusers strike. So it can hit you like a sucker punch. Victims of abusers don't set out to be abused. They start out by being nice to someone who had previously demonstrated very gracious social skills and appears to be having a bad week. But abusers are good arguers. They are good at manipulating other people into taking the blame. And then, after it goes on for a while, it gets absurd, and the victim doesn't buy into it anymore. But, by then, the abuser has arranged everything to make it hard for the victim to get out.

"In my case, I had to give up everything, except Stella and the clothes on my back. I was even scared about losing Stella, too. It was feasible. You see, abusers, they don't know when to quit. My ex-husband would've taken away the air that I breathed, if he could've figured out a way to get away with it. A really obsessed abuser won't quit short of death, if he's on a roll and getting his way. He used to tell me that I deserved to be punished for leaving him, yet, daily, he had screamed that Stella and I had ruined his life.

"Then he got into drugs. Maybe he'd always been into them and it only got worse. I'll never know. Drugs didn't make the situation bad in the first place, they just made it worse. And it gave me the tiniest opportunity of confusion in which to escape. If he'd suspected, he would've destroyed the car."

She described more frightening things to me, the smashing of cars in anger, the constant flattening of the tires. "I was just stupid, I guess. I mean, I just thought we had bad roads that ate the tires all the time. Afterwards, it took me a good five or six years without flats to figure out what had been going on. I mean, sometimes a set of tires wouldn't last me a week, and then he'd say I shouldn't drive any more, because I was costing too much in tires.

He wanted to keep me scared, scared to drive. He was scared I'd leave him. Of course, I wanted to. . . .

"But do you see how damaged abusers are, to even think of those things? Normal people don't think like that. So it's not that hard to become a victim, especially if you've got a personal history of always trying to work things out. That's how Indians are, mostly, you know—submissive. But I'm working on it. I'm really, really working on being anything but."

Indeed, she was.

CHAPTER NINETEEN
DOGS, HORSES, AND INDIANS ARE DEFENSELESS

Rachel's ex-husband had had her income imputed, for child support purposes, as though she was still working as a professional educator with a master's degree. And, even though he became delinquent in child support payments within the first year, he kept her afraid of taking him to court. She feared doing anything to put him in what she called "revenge mode." In an effort to keep her unemployed, and to guarantee that she would never be able to earn her fair share of the child support, he systematically contacted all of the school districts within an hour's drive of Little Rock.

Rachel survived by working as a substitute teacher. It was a low-paying job, and there was always a need. She was the only Indian in any of the school districts, and she took a lot of abuse. She put notes in all of her personnel files, indicating that she was to be contacted if odd correspondence appeared from Colorado. "But really, all it did was hurt me," she said. "Indians have got to be at least ten times better and more pure than whites in the field of education. It hurts. It really, really hurts."

One of the schools where Rachel subbed was Little Rock Elementary, the school that Stella attended, and the closest place Rachel could get a job. She was a very involved parent. She helped out in the classroom, helped coach Odyssey of the Mind, and helped with fundraising activities. Stella was a straight-A student and several grade levels above her classmates in reading. When teachers and bus drivers left notes for their substitutes, they would leave Stella's name as a student they could trust. Stella was happy.

But Stella's grades suddenly dropped. She began to panic when she heard the diesel engine of the school bus at the end of the driveway. She said, "No, no, I'm sick." Rachel thought it was just a normal childhood dip, and she kept putting Stella on the bus. Stella finally began throwing things, screaming, dropping herself in temper tantrums.

"It was like I finally got hit in the head with a baseball bat," said Rachel. I finally figured out that somebody was hurting my kid, and I said, 'What is happening at school?' You know, I was an educator, and I was an involved parent. I didn't think that somebody could be abusing my kid at school. Then it happened, even though I was doing everything right. The one thing I couldn't change was being colored, and because I was colored, I did not deserve the benefit of the doubt.

"Several letters had been sent to the school, by the father, asking that the school intervene in custody and visitation. And you know what? They did it! They *did* it! It's horribly unethical and illegal, but they did it.

"When I'd first come back here, I was so poor. All of my resources had gone into protecting Stella and me. I'd asked the people at school to help connect me with all of the institutional resources available. When I taught in the Southwest, we had clothing banks, warm coats, books, food programs, all sorts of resources available. The schools were so culturally diverse, that it had never occurred to me to discriminate or to evaluate people by their financial status. But, when I showed up here at Little Rock Elementary School, asking for help, I was labeled as low-income trash. I didn't realize that I was the first colored person to become a permanent resident in the school district. They had a few migrant kids now and then, and during that era, the ACLU would periodically sue the school on their behalf.

"The counselor and the principal began pulling Stella out of class and telling her that there was something wrong with her, because she didn't want to go to Colorado. She didn't want to go, because it was horrible. He was always high and drunk, and he'd go out and smash up the truck with a hammer. He'd block off her path to the bathroom, and she'd sneak out to pee inside of a big cedar tree when he was asleep.

"But her word didn't count. And my word didn't count. Because we were colored. Here was this white male, calling the shots. He said, 'Let's all us white folks jump together,' and they'd all jump."

As much as I disliked listening to this story, I could tell that Rachel disliked telling it. She hated the way they'd jumped to conclusions about her, had assumed that she was trash, without value. She had twice their credentials, but they never bothered to find that out, she said. She'd been sent out to substitute for them by a central Intermediate School District that had preapproved her credentials. They just jumped to conclusions, and this, she said, was the real racism in it all.

"If they'd only asked me, I'd have shown them my credentials. In fact, they actually had my credentials on file, but, you know, they'd probably gotten buried—or they didn't count. Or maybe my ethnic status outweighed my credentials. I'll never know the truth.

"The school counselor said, 'I can tell how much that poor man loves her by his letters. He said he didn't even know for sure if his little girl went to this school.' I was the one who had given him the name and address of the school. In fact, that information was in the divorce agreement. But they never asked me, they never talked to me, because I was the nigger in my neighborhood. I kept begging them to turn me in to social services. Legally, that's what they were supposed to do, if they were worried. But, I don't think they were worried about Stella. I think they were thinking about their own careers. It's like they were looking for some child abuse case to make themselves look great."

"What did the counselor have against you?"

"Don't know. I'd never met the woman."

I couldn't imagine Rachel letting someone treat her like that. *I* was always afraid of offending her.

The principal was brand new. He'd never been a principal before, and he'd only been on the job for three weeks. It was a freak situation. All three of the school district's previous administrators had left all at once, and the school board had to jump and fumble to fill the vacancies quickly, so that school could start. So they didn't check references well at all. But, actually, most school districts don't. By the early 1980s, eight out of ten educators were coming from the bottom 20 percent of the people in their high school graduating classes who went on to college. It's not a tough curriculum, so they all pull good grades. Even my own credentials are pretty fluffy.

Rachel had once told me that she'd taken fifty-seven college credits in one year, and that she kept up a 3.97 grade point average while she did it. If it was true, it made it easy to question the validity of my own credentials. Did Rachel or any other Indian have the right to tear down institutions that big, I couldn't help but wonder. So she was uncomfortable—was it any reason for hundreds of professionals to work overtime, or to give up bits and pieces of their own comfort levels? Wasn't Rachel being presumptuous? No, she'd told me, someone who works less than seventy hours a week cannot claim victimization by someone who does.

"So it turns out the new principal didn't have a very good reputation downstate where he was a teacher. They gave him good references to get rid of him. We had gotten burned in a game of 'pass the turkey.' And a lot of damage gets done in 'pass the turkey.' It takes many more years to undo damage than it takes the turkey to do it. Those taxpayers who get hurt in the process, they're real people with real needs, you know. And it's the weak who get hurt the most. And minorities are in that category of weak, you know. And just like other taxpayers, they're footing the bill for that system abuse.

"It's like the stories about Manaboozhou. He messes up sometimes, and all the generations that come after him have to live with the consequences of his mistakes. Most of the time, they're funny. But we've got tragic stories, too. Those are preventive, the tragic ones. How do you think we could have prevented this?"

"Prevented?"

"Prevented. The system. How can we fix the system?"

Sometimes her explanations and her issues got too big for me. It wasn't my story, and it was boring me. I certainly didn't want to fix the system. I had worked my way up through it. I hadn't gotten to know Stella yet, and I didn't have real faces to attach to Rachel's fear for her children. I just wanted to know about Indians and education. I didn't know she'd get so personal about all of it.

"So I asked them to stop what they were doing to Stella, because she was wetting herself and everything. She was really traumatized. Because of compulsory education laws, I figured I had to keep putting her on the train."

"What train?"

"Bus. I meant bus. . . . I guess I was young and stupid. I should have just kept her out of school until the county prosecutor got those people out of the building. But do you think he'd have even tried?"

"*Should* he have tried, Rachel?" It didn't seem worth the trouble or the expense to the taxpayers.

"They prosecute people for abusing dogs and horses. . . ."

Yes. Yes they do. But dogs and horses are defenseless.

CHAPTER TWENTY
SEPARATE IS NOT EQUAL

"But, you know, I was also just trying to be a normal person. I was trying to work things out. I asked them over and over to stop trying to change Stella's mind and to send the letters that started it all to the guardian in Colorado."

"Did they stop?"

"No. It was horrible, and she kept begging me to keep her out of school."

Perhaps she should have. After all, Rachel was a teacher. Why didn't she just homeschool Stella? Looking back at it now, in Rachel's shoes, I feel a twinge of guilt at having thought she should've sacrificed her right to a public education for her children. She paid more land taxes than most of her neighbors. No, Rachel wouldn't like that either; she'd say that 'one dollar one vote' was not an acceptable approach. She constantly pulled the rug out from under me with the idea that I was suppposed to look at her experiences with the public school system in terms of ethics. All I'd wanted were anecdotes.

"But I knew my legal rights a little bit," Rachel went on, "because I had been both a regular and special education teacher." Special education as we know it today was the result of a class action suit, Rachel had told me, so special education teachers really need to know the laws. That's a big part of the training.

"Parents and students have rights. So I went to the classroom teacher, and I told her that the counselor and the principal did not have my permission to take Stella out of the classroom.

"The next time they came for Stella, the classroom teacher refused to let her go. But they waited until she went to another teacher for social studies, and the other teacher let her go. Stella said they pulled her out by her clothes, and she dragged her feet and screamed and cried."

At this point Rachel was crying. "They hurt her. They've hurt her forever, you know. . . . She still talks about it, about what it's like to be trash in the white school system. That's why she's such an overachiever. Don't tell me there's not a dollar amount that a jury can't put on that kind of damage. They took away her childhood."

I hadn't met Stella yet. Back then I didn't have the image I have today of an adult in a child's body. Guilt. I felt it again. I like Stella. I prefer not to think of her as small and terrified and defecating on herself in her own driveway.

"My kids are turtles, you know."

"What?"

"Turtles."

"They're slow?"

"No. They're Turtles. Their clan, their guardian—Turtle Clan. Turtles are supposed to look out for other Turtles. But I was the only Turtle around, and I didn't do it. I didn't protect Stella. . . . Maybe if I'd lived closer to the reservation, there would have been other Turtles around to protect her. Maybe Indians should only live with other Indians. Maybe we shouldn't try to live in white communities. . . . But I really love Tall Man Jack, you know, and we can't pick up the farm and move it."

Actually, I didn't see why they couldn't have just picked up and moved. I hadn't seen the farm yet, the barns, the shelves, the carefully constructed systems by which they organized their lives. If the place had become so popular, I'd wondered, why didn't they move further north, where there were more Indians and fewer white people? Why did stubborn Rachel insist upon staying where she wasn't wanted and forcing her Ojibwe children and Ojibwe cultural values on a school district that didn't want them? But I knew what her answer would be, once I was there in her home, on her turf. She'd lean heavily on the word *public*, hiss out the word *taxes*, and wave her hand at the endless miles of cherry trees in tidy rows.

"Home." She'd say the word with rounded lips and rounded eyes, like a treaty lawyer, like a supreme court judge. It was a concept she held sacred.

"We'd come home from Colorado when Stella was little, and her name, it sounded kind of Spanish to them. . . . And when I'd filled out the enrollment forms at school, they'd asked if she knew another language, and I'd put Spanish. Because her day care givers spoke Spanish, and they'd taught Spanish to all the kids. It was Colorado, after all. Everybody taught their kids Spanish! I just thought she'd be helpful to her teacher with the migrant kids . . . that's why I let them know she knew Spanish. But to these guys, to these self-absorbed, small-minded people, she was icky, colored, Mexican. . . . It was anything goes. The laws didn't apply. Stella and I were expendable. I'm really careful when I fill out forms now. I don't tell them anything about the kids or our lives. School is not a safe place for colored children."

"Can't you send your kids to the tribal school?" I'd asked.

"And, if it closes?" she'd responded, and sure enough, the endeavor only lasted a year.

"I was born in nineteen fifty-four," she began, slowly. "There was an important Supreme Court decision back then. Perhaps you've heard of it? Brown versus the Board of Education?" She spoke to me cautiously, like she was a rattlesnake, unsure of whether or not she should strike.

"Separate is not equal. Ask the fish who huddle together in the oxygen-rich layers within the sun-warmed waters of an inland lake on an August afternoon. To deprive the minnows of oxygen would kill them. To rob the growing, larger predator fish of the opportunity to observe minnows would be detrimental to the survival of the larger species. Don't assume that bigger is better, or that that which is familiar to you is better for the well-being of your own personal pond."

Rachel dove back into her story. "So, I went in to the superintendent, and I was very nonthreatening about it. I just explained it, and said I wanted them to stop what they were doing to Stella.

"Anyhow, the superintendent was nice. He blurted out, 'Oh my god, that's illegal!' And he said he'd have them stop and he'd get the letters to me, so I could mail them to Stella's guardian in Colorado. I was scared to even have my fingerprints on them, so I gave the superintendent the address and asked him to do it. I was so used to being on the defensive. School administrators make pretty good money. My ex-husband could afford to jerk me around a lot, no matter what the cost, and he did."

"Did the superintendent send the letters?"

"No. Not at first."

"Why not?"

"Because he was a good administrator, and he gave them a chance to do things right themselves."

"Did they send the letters?"

"No. Instead the counselor made several phone calls to the guardian and talked him into resuming visitation and withdrawing from supervision. Those phone calls cost me almost two hundred dollars per hour—a full hour's worth of them."

"So Stella went out to Colorado?"

"No. As soon as my lawyer phoned me about it, I told her what had happened. So things went back into limbo, because she let the guardian know about the letters. The whole thing cost me more money than I was earning. It was awful. I almost couldn't afford to protect Stella. I thought about letting go of her and mourning her as though she were dead. I was that scared, you know. I was so used to being punished by my ex-husband. But I'd die without her. And her soul would've been eaten up in an abusive environment. That's what it does to children.

"Doing nothing is part of the chemistry of fear. We still don't know much about it yet. But, apparently, when a situation looks completely hopeless, it's not uncommon for a victim to just shut down. Fight or flight just quits working. It confuses the researchers, but it makes perfect sense to me. You can get killed quickly and painlessly, or you can suffer. It's that basic, that controlling, when someone abuses someone else.

"Abusers are good at selecting victims who are already weak and vulnerable. They don't pick people who are likely to fight back. So, even though it might be unusual that Stella and I would be abused by people in the schools, it made sense that we didn't have the skills or resources to protect ourselves yet when it did happen. We were underdogs. We were magnets for disaster."

Rachel was spewing out the whole story, and she didn't stop to lay blame. I wanted to know why she thought they were underdogs—was it because they were weak, or because they were Indians? She always seemed to confuse the two issues.

"So the guardian had to wait for the letters to arrive from the school before deciding about resuming visitation. Were they ever sent?"

"No! The superintendent had to intervene again. He finally sent them. And he must have had a pretty good talk with the counselor and the principal, because I got a call from the principal a few days later."

"What did he say?"

"He said that two more letters had arrived from Colorado, and that he'd be sending them on."

"Two more? It sounds pretty crazy."

"I was a sitting duck, unless I asserted my civil rights. Do you think that public schools should be that way? I mean, what happened to the *public* part of it? When did the needs of the people in power become more important than those of the less powerful members of the community? How do the emotionally scarred, the mentally impaired, the financially weak hold up in a system like this? How did it come to be here, in one of the fastest-growing areas of the state, where we should have our pick of the finest educators available? It is, after all, a profession that is supposed to be dedicated to public service, not personal and financial profit at all costs."

This felt too close, too personal. Time to steer her back to the letters. I was still curious. "So, were the new letters sent?"

"No."

It *was* getting pretty absurd. Maybe Rachel's anxiety about the school did have real foundation.

BENEFIT OF THE DOUBT

"No. No letters arrived in Colorado. I called the principal and asked him for a copy of the cover letter he'd sent with the letters. I didn't need to see the letters, I told him, just the date on the cover letter, because they hadn't arrived in Colorado yet, and it had been weeks. The guardian just wanted to know when to expect them. I really tried to be nice, even after everything. I'd thought things were going to work out. I was like that, you know, I just kept trying to be a good Indian. But it was too late, I was already dirt . . . and they were never going to let me be anything else."

"So they really hadn't been sent?"

"Probably not. Anyhow, it was about four-thirty on a Friday afternoon, and the building must have been almost empty."

"What do you mean?"

"The principal started screaming at me. I mean screaming. I could hear the echo in the room he was in, even over the phone. I could hear him spitting when he talked. I was glad I wasn't alone in a room with him."

"What did he say?"

"Fuu-uuck YOU! I don't have to send you a copy of my letter. Do I ask you to send me a copy of the letter every time you write to your kid's lawyer? NO! Do I have to send you a copy of anything I send to your kid's lawyer? NO. I can tell the guy anything I want. I'm fucking God! I can take your precious little girl away from you! You think you've got such big problems, you whiney little bitch? What about my problems? You went over my head, and you got my ass *ripped*!"

CHAPTER TWENTY-ONE

"You got my ass ripped?"

"Yeah, I never heard that one either," said Rachel. "Do you suppose he was talking about his anus?"

"Maybe. What else did he say?"

"Well, first I told him to calm down and take a deep breath, that I'd been a teacher, and that I knew that this wasn't the appropriate way to treat a parent."

"Did he stop?"

"No, he kept going. He said I deserved to be treated that way for going over his head. He said I deserved to be punished for it. Can you imagine the coincidence? Spooky!"

"Did anything happen after that?"

"I was scared to send Stella back to school. I called the superintendent the next Monday, but he just sounded annoyed and didn't have time to deal with it. Eventually, I had to send her back to school, I thought, or I'd get in trouble. Our parents used to get in trouble for not sending us to school, you know."

"Why wouldn't they send you?"

She ignored my question. "They made school a living hell for Stella."

"How?"

"She had to watch her step, constantly. One time she forgot her lunch, and they punished her."

"How?"

"They refused to let her have any food. Then they did a massive inquiry and blamed her for it, because she'd gone ahead and borrowed nickels and dimes from her classmates, then *bought* food from the same adults who'd turned her away. They interrogated each of the children who had loaned her money, behind closed doors, writing down everything those children said. How intimidating for them! Eventually, the principal found a five-cent discrepancy between what a nine-year-old child said she'd loaned Stella and how much Stella had said that the girl had loaned her. They said that that five-cent discrepancy was their out. Not guilty. Stella was the culprit, because she was smart, and didn't go hungry like that horrible monster of an administrator had wanted her to, just to punish me. Can you imagine her being forced to try to remember all those nickels and dimes adding up to the price of her lunch? Whenever Rachel complained, he took it upon himself to punish Rachel's child."

"Did they offer her bread and peanut butter?"

"No."

"I thought that was how they did it."

"That's how they do it for white kids whose parents don't complain. She tried to charge a lunch, but they wouldn't let her. She'd never charged a lunch in her life before. . . . She didn't have a backlog of charges or anything. Anyhow, it got bigger and uglier, in other ways, too."

"So she could never forget her lunch."

"Or anything. The office wasn't a safe place. Neither was the cafeteria. She couldn't afford for anything to go wrong. Could you imagine having to go to school under those circumstances every day?"

"No, I guess not."

"I mean, really, is this what this guy did with a significant chunk of his days, while the taxpayers provided him with a paycheck and dental benefits? I could imagine him hunched over his word processor, saying, 'I'm going to get you, Rachel, and your little dog, too!' But, she's not a dog, she's a child. She's flesh and blood, a parent's most prized possession. An administrator who would focus on punishing one parent and child like that is dangerous. I wouldn't have felt comfortable trusting him with my dog. Is that a satisfactory relationship between parent and school?"

But really, I wasn't sure. It was just one lunch, after all. Maybe Rachel was just paranoid about whites. Maybe she was just paranoid about public school administrators. For all I knew, she was lying abut what a good kid Stella was. I knew from experience that a lot of parents thought their children could do no wrong.

"Where is that administrator now, Rachel?" I asked her.

"I believe that that particular turkey is being passed up and down the coast, even as we speak. Just follow the blood-red trail of cranberry sauce. Not exactly what you'd call a yellow brick road. . . ."

It had been another futile phone call. I was still working on my thesis back then. All I'd wanted Rachel to do was give me a few pages about her experiences with the schools. I'd wanted summaries, that was all. But she'd insisted that drawing conclusions was my job, not hers. She said she'd already sorted through it all, and that now it was my turn to decide who should get the benefit of the doubt and who should not. I was leaning toward the school staff and a big misunderstanding, but then I remembered the other two letters, and I wondered what had happened to them.

CHAPTER TWENTY-TWO
THE STALKING

"So what happened to the other two letters?" I asked Rachel.

"Not even close."

"What?"

"We're not even close to being there yet."

"There's more?"

"Things got stranger and stranger. Finally, my neighbor mentioned some of these problems to a fellow she went to church with, who happened to be on the school board. We spoke, and I told him as much as I could figure out.

"Then I got connected with the president of the school board, and she and I met in the superintendent's office. She was really nice. She said, 'And we can assure this woman that no one will threaten her child again.' And all kinds of stuff was supposed to happen. The principal was supposed to go into anger management counseling, and I was supposed to be reimbursed for the illegal phone calls the counselor had made. The principal was supposed to stay away from Stella, too.

"But none of that happened. I'd asked for so little, too. . . . I mean, in the long run, it had cost me a small fortune. It took more than one lawyer to sort it out, and I ended up making all kinds of concessions on child support, because I was still scared of my ex-husband, and the school principal now, too. It was horrible. . . . He started to stalk me."

"Your ex-husband?"

"No, he was already stalking me. I'll have to show you the letters he claimed he sent to the IRS. They're hysterical. Even better are the ones he supposedly sent to INS."

"INS?"

"Immigration and Naturalization Service."

"But, you're a Native American."

"Yeah. That's what's so funny about it."

"So who stalked you?"

"The elementary school principal."

"Your daughter's elementary school principal stalked you?"

"Uh huh."

"Why do you think he'd do that? Was it sexual?"

"No way. Power. Just power. I didn't buy into his nice-guy-on-the-surface routine. He'd already blown it and shown his real self to me, the ugly one, the abused child. I was dangerous to him, and so he pulled out all the stops. I guess he thought that shutting me up was the key to his success. But, you know what? It didn't matter. His bosses didn't care what he did to Rachel and her children, because we were colored. We were expendable."

Rachel scared me, sometimes. She could be so direct. I could see how she might frighten people, if they weren't being up front themselves.

"Do you have traditional stories about stalking?" Maybe something useful would come out of this conversation, after all.

"Of course, we have traditional stories about everything. But they're not pretty ones, the ones about abuse of power. Not all of our stories are pretty. We do not exist strictly for your entertainment or to reinforce your sense of national history. We are living, breathing, *intelligent* flesh."

My questions had offended her. She knew that I wasn't giving her the benefit of the doubt, either. Her story was too bizarre.

"Did you go back to the school board?"

"Well, I'd found that people don't respond too well when you complain to them more than once. They get annoyed. They think you are being a pest because you got their attention. They give the benefit of the doubt to the white male administrator. That's what the superintendent had done."

"I see."

"I mean, I tried. School board members are state officials. They're supposed to be responsible if they know that someone is breaking the law in their schools. I told two different people on the school board how he was stalking me, but they didn't believe me."

"They didn't believe you?"

"Would you?"

"No, I guess not."

"He'd said to me, 'Go ahead and complain. No one will ever believe you.' And he was right."

"I can see how that might happen."

"Yeah. It was scary. It started out with him driving back and forth past my house over and over one weekend. Then, every time I went to a store or someplace, during the hours that school was out, he'd show up in line behind me. And then he started following me to my jobs at night. And he kept driving by on weekends. One time, I was demonstrating in a museum in Traverse City, and a docent came up to me and said, 'Excuse me, there's a man following you around.' He was nice, and he walked my daughter and me out to our car when it was time to go. It went on for months and months. He wrote to me, too."

"He wrote to you?"

"Three times a week, on average. On school stationery, with his name in big letters on the top. I think his name was in larger type than the name of the school. He'd periodically drift into delusions of power, I suppose. Bigger was better. He was kind of short. Maybe that had something to do with it. When I was at Oberlin College, we used to play volleyball in the courtyard at the dorm, and this one short kid was really aggressive. He just ruined the game for me, because he never gave me a chance. He was so insecure. . . ." I could visualize Rachel sticking her hand into her vest, like Napoleon.

"What did he say?"

"He'd gotten my resume out of the old personnel file and had gone over it with a fine-toothed comb. He was writing about the details in my resume, saying how impressive they were. He was writing about details in Stella's days at school. He was interviewing the staff about her, the other children, third and fourth graders, pulled into his office alone and interviewed about one little Indian kid. Can you imagine? I was scared for her. There was no guardian ad litem for us, although you'd think that's what the school board members should be for the public. But not my children. . . ."

"Creepy!"

"When you know the circumstances that came beforehand, yes, very creepy."

"Three times a week?"

"By certified mail. I've kept them in a big file, in case the swill ever hit the fan. Bizarre, that any one parent should have to keep a file of interactions in self-defense. It's not what you'd call a user-friendly system, is it?"

"No, I guess not."

"Other stuff happened, too. Before that, Stella was the first one on the school bus and the first one off. Then they changed it, so she was the first one on AND the last one off. The bus driver kept trying to change it, but they wouldn't let him. But she's amazing, you know, fifteen hours a week on the bus, and she just adapted. She's always got her homework done by the time she gets off of the bus. She makes Isabel do hers, too. She gets A's. She's amazing."

"How did you get the stalking to stop?"

"I just disappeared, went completely underground. I quit taking jobs locally during the hours that school was out. I worked in the Upper Peninsula a lot. I quit having anything to do with school. I quit going to parent-teacher conferences. I quit helping with teams and fundraisers. I didn't watch her at school concerts any more, or the school play. Sometimes I'd sneak in and watch the rehearsals, after she was in junior high, when I thought it might be safe. I'd hide the Tercel way back in the parking lot, behind a truck or something. I didn't want to cross his mind. I figured he was feeling pretty powerful, to do the things he'd been doing, and to be reinforced by his employers like that. They kept him for five years after that, you know."

I couldn't imagine a school district keeping an employee after those sorts of complaints. As a former administrator, I couldn't imagine being sued by the ACLU. How could communication between a school and a community break down to the point that something like that would be tolerated? Rachel claimed it was about fear for real estate values, hiding problems to keep up the Mayberry effect. She insisted that most people in Little Rock didn't think of abuse against coloreds as a problem. They were more likely to advocate prosecuting an animal abuse case.

"There were phone calls then, too."

"He phoned you?"

"We don't know who. They'd hang on for a while, then hang up. There was no caller ID in rural areas yet. The sheriff's department gave us a line trap on our telephone, but the calls were coming from a phone booth in a

105

town about seven miles from here. Eventually, they quit, when caller ID became commonplace."

"Do you have caller ID now?"

"I don't even have touch tone. I don't even have an answering machine."

"I know. I hate it."

"I'd never call you back, anyways. I told you, I'm a recluse."

"So what happened to the other two letters?"

"Superintendent confiscated them and sent them to Colorado."

"And?"

"Stella never had to go to Colorado again. The ex was forbidden from contacting the school or the house or Stella. It was a great burden off of all of our backs. But, we still had that principal to be scared of. And even after he left, he'd been such a strong mentor to the other principal, who eventually became the new superintendent, that we feel like the abuse never stopped. We feel like he's carried a grudge for his buddy."

"Why?"

"I don't know—the code of the good ol' boys, I guess. When I was still teaching, the field of education was 80 percent female, but the administrators were 80 percent male.

"The field of education is 89.3 percent white. This does not reflect the population of this state. If you draw a line across this state one-third of the way up, there are no Indians teaching outside of tribal schools."

"Why can't you teach at a tribal school?"

"Gee, Massa, you don't think I'm good enough to teach at y'all white folks' schools? I got the highest scores in the country on the National Teacher Exam. Not the highest scores for colored people, not the highest scores for monkeys, the highest scores for *human beings*. I'm sorry, you still looking for someone with a *higher* score to teach *white* children? Education is not an integrated field here; when are you going to figure it out?"

"I didn't mean that."

"I'm certain I heard you drawl when you said that. What did you say, you spell your name with a KKK?"

"OK, I earned that."

"Maybe a little. But you've got to think about Brown versus the Board of Education. Separate is not equal. Actually, sometimes together is not equal either, if staff and community expectations are not equal. No colored teachers. Kids get the idea at an early age that coloreds don't belong culturally in important jobs in important places like schools. Whoa . . . whazzat? Did I just see a bunch of knees jerk? You want the best teachers for your children? Maybe racist models are not the best thing for your children. Maybe white kids get hurt by racism in the system, too. Maybe *all* kids suffer when a good minority teacher is passed up for a white job candidate with fewer skills and less experience. . . . Indians, we couldn't afford to send our bottom 20 percent to college. We sent our top 20 percent."

I knew what she was talking about. It was one of the first statistics I had learned in my first basic education course at the university: 80 percent of the people who went into the field of education came from the bottom 20 percent of the people in their high school graduating class who went on to college. But *I* wasn't one of *those*.

"So why don't Indians do something about it?"

"Where have you been? We get in trouble if we just say, 'Please stop breaking the law and abusing our children.'"

"Maybe you should get more aggressive."

"Maybe *you* should get more aggressive."

"Why me, Rachel?"

"You don't understand. We didn't grow up the way you did. Your dad could drink a beer on his front porch. Mine couldn't. You could celebrate your religious conventions freely when you were a kid. We couldn't. It was outlawed. And those laws were foolishly kept on the books until the mid-seventies. We had to deal with the FBI all the time. We've been scared, scared for generations. And when we do speak up, do people like you believe us? Or do you get angry at us for trying to change the status quo?

"The Indian boarding schools in this state didn't close until twenty-two years after Brown versus the Board of Education. They didn't close nationwide until 1988; that's thirty-four years after 'Separate is not equal.' Actually, I found out that the last Indian boarding school was in Michigan, on one of the islands, but they kept it going into 1990 by claiming that it was open to non-Indians, too. It was a publicly and privately funded reform school. They tried to send one of my cousins there in 1989, from a school district up there closer to the reservation. But I kept telling his mom to refuse to sign the papers. So they put Frankie in special education instead. When I was a substitute teacher, I used to see him on the bus, when I'd load the kids in wheelchairs. He'd look down, in shame, but I'd always catch his eye and blow him kisses."

CHAPTER TWENTY-TWO

"Where is he now?'

"He blew his brains out, at the age of sixteen."

"Oh . . . Don't you think counseling might have helped a boy like that Rachel?"

"What that boy needed was economic and social equality, not counseling, not special education. You can't just fix the symptoms, not when you know the source of the infection, especially if you know it's fixable. He was a math nerd. Can you imagine, a boy who could look at a geometric configuration and predict its formula, and they had him doing times tables. He used to break his pencils."

"They treated my Isabel that way, too. But we were lucky, because one of the teachers figured it out. Before that, I would just tell her to shut up and play dumb, because I taught her everything she needed to know when we were up in the bush, by candlelight."

"Like Lincoln."

"Do you know what he's famous for to us?"

"Freeing the slaves?"

"Hanging Indians. Thirty-eight of them. I've heard it was even in the Guinness Book of World Records, as the largest mass execution in U.S. history. For us, it's stayed alive in our oral history. It happened just on the other side of the big lake, you know."

"That was then."

"And now is now. I know you don't care about this stuff, but it has real repercussions. If you're going to write about Indians and problems with the education system, you've got to stop using past tense."

And I did, when I wrote my thesis. I don't think I was as convinced as Rachel, but I did point out that problems still exist. But Rachel—I was sure she wasn't going to forgive me for not using the word *sociopathy*.

CHAPTER TWENTY-THREE
CULTURAL APPROPRIATION

S o, now I was supposed to try to figure out how what happened to Stella determined whether or not Rachel's neighbors were racists. My cocoa was syrupy and thick at the bottom.

"Can Zoey measure?"

"In a pinch. She gets all A's and B's at school. She just doesn't *want* to measure right now. Besides, it's good for them to not measure sometimes. Sometimes failure is as important as success."

"So, how does the whole Stella thing tie in to what these people might think of you?"

"Do you see it happening to them?"

"No, I guess not. But how does it make them racists?"

"Do you see them doing anything about it?"

"I don't know."

"No, no . . . These are the people who become school board members. These are the people who work less than seventy hours a week. These are the ones who can get involved somehow, who can get laws changed, policies changed, but they don't. They hang Indian artwork over their fireplaces and consider themselves radicals for doing it.

"They know about what happens to Stella and me. I don't keep secrets. But, they're happy, as long as it doesn't happen to them. Jeez, did you see the side of Z's head this morning? But, even when confronted with physical evidence, the school powers will choose to dump on me instead, with no evidence. They perceive those people as powerful, and they don't want to ruffle their feathers. They want their paychecks to stay high and steady. It's the American way."

"But Rachel, I've been here for a week. Tall Jack has shown me the maps. You own *miles* of waterfront property, compared to these people's feet of it. Miles! You probably own at least a hundred acres for every acre that they own. . . . *You* are powerful, too!"

"Not to them, yet. It takes lawsuits to make them think, to get past their stereotypes. Think about it. The history of education is a history cemented in Supreme Court decisions. It is a very slow process. Schools don't just automatically comply. Legislation follows, then more lawsuits, when the legislation is not complied with."

"Isn't that because school districts are so poor?"

"School administrators are the highest-paid officials in this county—and among the most poorly educated."

"Rachel, I can't believe you're saying this!"

"You're the one with the doctorate in education. Statistics don't lie."

And she was right. Statistics don't lie. They just get hidden, obfuscated. Obfuscated? Where did I pick up that word? I was starting to talk like Rachel. I didn't want to be Rachel. I didn't want to agree with Rachel. Rachel was angry. I didn't need controversy or anger in my life or in my book. I was looking for something noble to write about, and Rachel was overstepping her bounds by shoving all this crap at me first.

"You know, maybe public school administrators should have to take psychological exams, just like police officers. Even the Catholic church is starting to recognize abuse and is considering psychological profiling for people in contact with children.

"People in general get a response to authority when they walk through the door of a school building. It's part of the hierarchy required for crowd control. But, we, as educators, have an obligation to not abuse those responses to subliminal power that are forced on all of us as children. Do you know what I mean?"

I think I did understand a little bit. I did understand the knee-jerk reaction to authority that people get when they walk through the door of a school. Rachel was the first person I'd ever met to talk openly about it, to point out that it was necessary, for crowd control. But she also questioned how we drew limits on the authority that we gave to public school employees. Through legislation, she'd insisted. Things are complicated for good reasons. She was the first person I'd ever met who thought that complication was OK.

It also surprised me to realize that, throughout all of this, Rachel had somehow managed to maintain her self-identity as an educator. Part of what had happened to her was that the local school authorities did *not* recognize her credentials. In their minds, her socioeconomic status outweighed her skills and training.

But it took me years to give Rachel the benefit of the doubt, too. I didn't consider her an educator until I'd realized how hard-working she was, how she'd accumulated real estate, how she volunteered in her community. Even when I'd watched her woo rooms full of college personnel and community leaders, I still thought of her as an expert on Indian things only, on Indian education only. I was discomforted by her anger at and criticism of the system. It was *my* system, my identity.

"I don't want to hear about how much you hate the educational system, Rachel. I'm done with my thesis. I want to hear about the traditional stories and how they tie in with your life."

"This *is* about the traditional stories!" Rachel rose up out of her chair, and the cat leapt away.

"Traditional stories are about real-life issues! They sing, praise, desecrate, and tear apart ideas!" She was pacing the living room, from the paper-covered dining table to the toy-strewn couch.

"So, you want warm and fuzzy and pretty, so you can print some sort of cheesy children's book about tricksters! Shame on you! Shame on you for thinking that our stories are that shallow. Shame on you for thinking that you can edit them, shorten them, can them into your own stereotypical visions of what Indians are supposed to be like in your warped view of American history!"

This was getting personal. I was not racist. I was *here*. I . . .

"So, you think you should be patted on the back for being merely *interested* in Indian stuff? You're here to make money off of it. But you don't know how to do anything but fit it into *your* needs. We need these stories to fit into *our* needs. Do you think every Indian in this state owns real estate? Number one highest unemployment—what part of that don't you understand? That's a statistic produced by the state board of education. Didn't you read any of that stuff, when you worked on your doctorate in this state? And if you did read it, didn't you process it?

"Stella tells me all the time: 'Mom, quit trying to fix the world, just take care of yourself.' And I get mad at her for it! 'Stop emulating them, Stella,' I tell her. I hate to get all Noam Chomsky on you, but don't you think that maybe we have an obligation to improve things a little bit?

"I mean, Jeez, here we are educators. Isn't it supposed to be about creatively putting ideas out there about improving the human condition? Teaching by example. It's not just supposed to be about getting a good-paying job with good benefits.

"And it's sure as Hell not about stealing stories from a bunch of underpaid and powerless Indians and making money off of them. Haven't you ever heard the term 'cultural appropriation'?"

"No."

"It's what you're trying to do—to *me*. I am not stupid. I know exactly what you are trying to do. And I'm fighting back. I'm educating you. I'm taking the time to educate you, because I'd had hope for you, that maybe you could go out and graciously educate your peers. Who's going to bring the field of education into the twenty-first century? I don't have time to educate each and every one of you one at a time. I've got a life to live. I've got babies to cuddle. I've got peaches that ripen all at once, and the smell of a full and warm peachy kitchen full of canning jars to live. You can't have any more of my time! Especially if you can't stop looking for your dream story, your meal ticket."

The phone rang, and I felt relieved. She pulled the short cord into the bedroom and shut the door. The phone barely hung cockeyed on the wall.

Rachel stomped out of the bedroom and rummaged through the refrigerator. She lobbed a carton of eggs at the counter. I looked around the house and listened quietly. I was fairly certain the children were hiding. I heard muffled giggles coming from the bedroom.

"Isabel!" Rachel barked out. "Chop onions, now!"

CHAPTER TWENTY-FOUR
THE SOCIAL WORKER

"D̶o you want to know who that was on the phone?" Rachel was chopping, sorting, staring at me for the first time since I'd met her.

"OK."

"It was a social worker. Some social worker, calling me from her car phone. She wants to do a children's book, and she wanted me to tell her a rabbit story right then and there."

"You didn't, did you?"

"No. I gave her a lecture on cultural appropriation, just like I just gave you.

"I hate teaching you people one at a time. This is what the schools and the universities are supposed to be doing. That's why you're supposed to teach about minorities, even little bitty minorities, like Indians. And it's not just supposed to be warm and fuzzy, like you want. It's supposed to have ugly and boring details, whether you like it or not. It's to try to cut down on the amount of abuse against minorities that *still* happens, on an everyday basis.

"I mean, this woman actually thought it was OK to steal an Indian story and make money off of it! And she thinks so little of Indians, that she thinks she can write down an Indian story accurately. And she thinks so little of Indians, that it's OK to steal intellectual property from us. She thinks so little of Indians, that she thinks that federal copyright laws don't apply to us. And she thinks so little of *me*, that she thinks it's OK to waste my time and steal from me personally. And she's a *social worker*—for Little Rock County! She probably thinks she's really lucky to have this job where she's in contact with Indians, so she can learn about us and get ideas for her children's books. *That's* why I don't have an answering machine! She'd have expected me to call her back, long distance, up in the north end of the county, and tell her a sweet little story at *my* expense. . . .

"I *hate* educating you people one at a time!"

And she chopped. And she washed the bowls and utensils as she worked. And she washed them faster than I'd ever seen a human being wash dishes.

Tall Jack came in. I could hear him taking off his snowshoes and leaning them against the side of the house. He was wearing those immense, round boots. He didn't take them off, but unzipped his overalls from the ankle up, as far as he could, to let air circulate around his pantlegs. "Hot in here!" he'd commented.

"I heard you out there, tapping ice. How was it?"

"Damage to maybe one in twenty-five," she said, almost pleasantly.

"Not bad. Could've been worse."

Rachel fished three bags of corn chip remnants from the top of the refrigerator. Each one was rolled up and clipped shut with a clothespin. She removed the clothespin from each and violently crushed its contents with the heels of her hands. She shook the bags' contents into a frying pan full of sizzling onions and garlic. Then she literally began throwing all the leftovers in the refrigerator into the pan. Plastic containers and lids were heaped furiously into the sink, where they bobbed responsively in the dishwater. She dumped a half pint of pickled jalapeños into a bowl of eggs, whipped them up at the speed of light, and drizzled the bowl guts over the steaming mass.

I sat next to Tall Jack, on the couch, with a full plate. I'd come to recognize the theme songs that were played regularly on The Weather Channel.

Jack looked over at me. "She scare you?"

"Yes."

"Deserve it?"

"I think so."

He laughed out loud, and scooped a chunky forkful of omelette into his mouth.

The kids entertained themselves for the rest of the day by waiting until Lala fell asleep on a bed, and dropping a potato chip on the floor. At Rachel's suggestion, they taped a large chart to the living room wall and graphed how many tries it took to get the soft sound to wake the dog from a dead sleep.

CHAPTER TWENTY-FIVE
EQUINOX

It was spring equinox, "a turning point," Rachel had called it. A wet, warm snow was falling. It was thick and beautiful, and it had covered the tops of the white spruce that ran like sentinels around Rachel's house and yard. The cherry trees, in the distant orchard, seemed small and spindly in comparison. But Rachel's yard was hugged in by huge trees in every direction, like a sanctuary. She really was a recluse.

The family had been sent out to school and work, and the house was quiet. I could hear the logs crackling inside the cast-iron woodstove. I finally figured out why Rachel's house was so quiet. There was no furnace, no blowers going off and on. The refrigerator was not self-defrosting, so there was no fan. It was about seven thirty in the morning, and the light outside was flat. It felt good to drink hot coffee and watch the heavy snow in such a silent atmosphere. A ladybug crawled across my pantleg above the knee.

Rachel was bringing in armloads of firewood. It was a regular post-school bus ritual that she performed. She said it warmed her up and got her heart pumping. I'd helped her bring some in once. The wood was a lot heavier than I'd imagined, and it made my back sore. I understood why Stella only brought in the larger pieces one at a time. The gloves I'd been given had stiff plastic palms, and it was hard to pick up the wood. The wood was stacked, split down, in tall ricks built on top of old shipping palettes, so that they could be moved with a forklift on the back of a tractor. The ricks had tops made of roofing metal, so that snow didn't bury the wood. But, the day I helped, an inch of snow had blown into the ricks, and each piece of wood had to be brushed clean before it was picked up. The wood was down to the bottom of the rick, and I had to bend for every single piece. When I got to the bottom layer, each piece had patches of thick, white webbing on its underside, and Stella showed me how to brush them off with a pine cone. "We don't want the spiders in the house," the child said, making a face, and threw the pine cone over a rick into the woods.

That piece of woods sheltered Rachel's house from the road. A hundred feet back from the ricks, I noticed a tall tree that had an unusual spiral-shaped trunk. It stood alone in a small clearing. It was as though the forest around it had been groomed. I asked Stella what kind of a tree it was.

"Rachel?"

"What?"

"Rachel. She's a white pine."

"You name your trees?"

"Just Jack and Rachel." The child huffed and shuffled into the mud-room with her wood. I waited for her to come back out.

"What are you talking about?"

"The trees. There were two of them, grown together. Some kid probably just twisted them up together like that thirty years ago and tied them up so they'd grow that way."

"I only see one of them."

"Jack died."

"Oh. Where is he now?"

Stella pointed to several twisted chunks of firewood rotting in a pile between two trees. "There. We don't burn pine. Gums up the stovepipe."

"The trees were intertwined?"

"Yeah. That's why we named them Jack and Rachel."

"Was Jack a red pine?"

"Yup. My dad cut him down. Had to use his special chain saw on a pole. It was a lot of work to save Rachel. He's like that."

"Like what?"

"Well, ya gotta love 'im."

"I see."

Now, when Rachel made a pass through the mudroom, filling the big woodbox, I called out, "Where would a ladybug come from on a day like this?"

"Firewood," she called back, "like the spiders." Then she pointed up at the beams. I looked up and noticed the cobwebs for the first time.

"How do you get rid of the webs?"

"Tall Man Jack bought me a special telescoping tool for Christmas one year. Feel free to use it."

"Do you want help with the firewood?"

"No, I'm almost done. Gonna get cold, you know."

When the snow briefly changed to rain, Rachel stopped bringing in wood and brushed off a couple of the Tercels with a big push broom. She hung her down vest to dry near the woodstove. She took the old percolator from the top of the stove, gave it a shake, and went to the kitchen, where she added wild mint tea from a canning jar in the refrigerator.

"Coffee was kind of strong this morning," she said, after returning the pot to the woodstove to reheat. She settled in, with her damp sneakers close to the open stove door. She looked at peace, and it seemed a good time to try to get stories out of her.

"You seem to like your routine."

"I suppose I do."

"Heating with wood is more work than I thought."

"You only see the half of it. Tall Jack does the hard part, cutting, splitting, hauling it around with the tractor. It dries over there in the barnyard. Then, after two years, he brings it here. If you think it's heavy now, you should feel it when it's green! Stella and I help Tall Jack load it onto the back of the tractor in the woods. Stella does it now, more than me, because Little Jack can't be out there. He wouldn't stay far enough away from the axe or the pile where Tall Man tosses the split pieces.

"Tall Jack likes doing that firewood, though. It's OK to like your work. It's OK to not separate work from life. A lot of people are happy with what they do."

"Are you happy with what you do?"

"Sometimes. Sometimes I love the physical labor of the farm, but sometimes there's too much for me. It can be back-breaking. All that pruning. You know, it's hard on Tall Jack's neck. He pulls muscles sometimes, but he can't stop, because the work has to be done. It's like that with picking up the brush, too. All those branches that are pruned off of the trees, they've got to be sorted and dealt with."

"How do you sort them?"

"First, we wait for the snow to melt. Just a few more weeks now, then it'll get crazy. We'll work as fast as we can. We cut the little branches off of the big ones, and we toss the fat, branchless limbs in between the trees, in piles, so we can pick them up later, with a trailer on the back of a Tercel. The kids can do that. They learn to drive before they ever get to a road with their learner's permit. Even Isabel can drive. But Miz Z, she's not ready yet, maybe next year. She can't concentrate yet. The fat branches are the firewood you see in the barn, for the workshop and for skating.

"You get blisters cutting those little branches off. We use huge nippers, like this." She held out her arms. "We use them to cut the feet off when we're butchering deer. They could really hurt you. I have to take out toy trucks and things for Little Jack to play with, so he can go up and down the rows and stay far away from me and the tool. It's just a precaution. I'm a little bit crazy that way, I guess.

"See those grassy rows between the cherry trees? We pile up all the smaller branches on those rows. We have to interweave them a little bit, so they don't blow away, because it takes weeks to do all of them. There are miles and miles of rows. We only pile up the branches that are smaller in size than a fifty-cent piece. That's about what the mower can safely handle. Then, when it's a nice, dry day, Tall Jack will drive up and down the rows with the tractor and mow them. It's not like a lawn mower; it's called a Brush Hog. Farming is very industrial, you know."

No, I didn't know, but I was learning. Rachel stuffed a fat piece of birch into the stove, swung the door shut, and clipped it shut with her tool.

"I don't see many birch trees here on the farm. Where do you get birch?"

"We have a couple of thousand acres north of here that we're putting a logging road into. It's a slow process, because we're doing it all ourselves, by hand. There's no hurry. The trees have been there forever, and we'll only take a few at a time. If you do it right, your grandchildren can log the same piece of property that you log. It's not about quick profits, you know. It's about them, your babies, setting them up for the kind of life you want for yourself."

"How do you know they'll want to do what you do?"

"You don't. But it's nice to give them the option. They're making more people all the time, but they're not making more real estate, or more lakes, or more trees. You're an educator. You're supposed to know these things."

119

"It seems like just sitting by this fire, making baskets, would be a nice way to live."

"How often do you see me sit?"

"Not often, I guess."

"Once, I applied for this job. . . . They were desperate. School started in a week. But my application disappeared, and they hired somebody on a waiver with only a bachelor's degree. It was a Spanish teaching job. And the guy they hired had never had a single class in Spanish. The parents were pretty upset, but the superintendent just told everybody that they couldn't find a teacher who knew Spanish."

At that point, Rachel flew into a long tirade in Spanish. I'd studied enough of the language in college to know that Rachel was better at it than me. It made sense; she'd taught in the Southwest, where she needed to use the language regularly in the classroom.

"Do you think it was racial discrimination?"

"Sort of."

"What do you mean?"

"I was labeled as a troublemaker, because I'd tried to stop them from hurting my daughter."

"But, they were breaking the law by talking to Stella like that and by talking to that lawyer like that."

"Most parents don't know that."

No, most probably didn't.

"I still hurt, you know, because I let them hurt Stella. It was my job to protect her. I am her mommy. It hurts me more when they hurt my kids than when they hurt me. And it still hurts my kids, because there is no lee-way for them, no margin of error that any child should have in a safe educational environment. And they know that their mom is colored, and viewed as less in the community. They hate being part Indian. If everybody didn't already know that they were, they'd claim to be something else—Italian maybe. Me too, wish I could change it all. . . .

"Anyhow, it was racial discrimination that made them hurt Stella in the first place. And it was second-phase racial discrimination that made them hire someone with a fragment of my credentials, because I wasn't a nigger who stayed in her place."

She used the word "nigger" so freely. I cringed every time she used it. It was so politically incorrect. She'd tried to explain it to me once, that she thought that it was a heavily loaded term that deserved a place in twenty-first-century civil rights issues. "To refuse to use the word is to deny that the concept exists," she'd said. "We still live in a very stratified society.

"And it's probably age discrimination, too," Rachel went on.

"How do you mean?"

"It's cheaper to hire somebody with a bachelor's degree than somebody with my credentials."

"But, they're supposed to hire the person with the best credentials."

"Not if you're the superintendent, and your next raise is based upon how much money is left over in the budget."

"That's awful."

"No, that's the way the system works. An independent firm does studies about how much money per dollar each school district spends per student. It's compared to state test scores. Don't ask me about state test scores. Don't get me going about how people manipulate the system. It needs to be revamped every few years, to close up the loopholes, just like every other bureaucracy in the world. Government is a living organism. . . ."

"Does Stella get good test scores?"

"Best in the state. She's got awards, from the governor, from outside agencies. All of her awards and praise come from outside the school system. That's why she works with all those different charities and outside programs. She's learned that the school has nothing to offer her, no matter how hard she works. She's been labeled. She's one of Rachel's children."

CHAPTER TWENTY-SIX
A SINGLE FEATHER

It was one of the longest weeks in my life, that first time I was at Rachel's house. Sometimes it was too busy, too full, and other times it was interminably dull. Sometimes I had to do things like watch her scrape the plaque off of her dog's teeth, before she'd give me the time of day. I had to play Uno with her kids.

I finally figured out that she and Tall Man Jack did have quite a love life going. It had seemed, at first, that they barely spoke. But I saw them a few times, reflected in the living room windows, while I was watching an evening special on tornadoes and other violent weather systems. They would stand, pressed together, shirts lifted up, arms around one another, behind the kitchen counter. I'm certain that the kids saw them, too. But none of them showed it.

Sometimes Little Jack would drop everything, leap up, and run into the bedroom, screaming, "Body slam, body slam! No! Me first! I'm stealing your body slams, Dad." Other times, the boy would whisper loud and wet into Rachel's ear, "Can I have body slams and we'll tell Dad about them, and he'll feel bad, 'cause I got more than him?" He'd probe under her shirt, and she'd grab his hand and kiss it.

Sometimes Rachel sat brooding, working on small baskets. She was famous for her sweetgrass baskets. She loved making them, but she had to be in the mood, she said. And it hurt her arm if she did too much at one time. The repetitive stress from the repeated tight motions of sewing the small, fragrant grass bundles would cause her to hold her arm straight up over her head. I'd suggested doing a book about making baskets, but she wouldn't even consider it. "No, no. I can market the mystery," she insisted. "It's the only work I've got that's mine. No one will hire me, you know, except my husband. He doesn't know how to hate an Indian, especially this one."

I saw her yell at the kids, send them running, cuddle them, woo them, educate them. I learned that Tall Jack spent as much valuable time with them as Rachel did. One day, he took Little Jack and me for a walk in the national lakeshore. He drove only seven or eight minutes from the house. Then we walked up an isthmus between two lakes, one on the north and one on the south. Both were covered with ice. The one on the south was not safe to walk on. Tall Jack took a small dead tree in his hands and banged out on the ice fringes as far as he could. The wet edges gave way into thick chunks.

Then we cut across a narrow part of the isthmus to the northern lake. Its edge was in the shade and frozen solid to the shore. Tall Jack stepped out gingerly, then urged Little Jack to follow. I followed, too, but he instructed me to stay away. "We've got to spread out, keep from concentrating our weight in one spot." I realized that what we were doing was risky. It had been too warm and sunny, off and on, for us to trust the ice. It took a long time before Tall Jack let go of Little Jack's hand and let him wander off across the ice, to a spot where small bushes protruded. I was glad I'd brought my sunglasses. There was little wind, and I was almost warm, with the sunlight reflecting up at me from every surface. The ice surface rose and fell like gently rolling hills. I had expected it to be flat.

We came to a small channel between the lakes. Jack cautioned me not to step on its snowy surface. "It has a pretty good flow," he warned. We kept going, and then I realized we were in a swamp. I followed the two of them, grabbing on to small trees and looking for dry footholds. Then we came to a larger channel with a clear running stream. Lala was swimming, drinking the water as she paddled. We couldn't cross the bigger stream, so we backtracked.

We drove a few miles to a different place. And then we walked for miles, climbing hills and sand dunes. We were close to Lake Michigan, and there wasn't much snow. We saw at least a hundred deer in the swamps and some sandhill cranes. Tall Jack could recognize the calls of the various waterfowl that passed overhead.

We found a place where a blue jay had died. Nothing was left but the feathers. Little Jack picked them up, along with some huge acorns. He handed them to me, saying, "Here, keep them in your pocket. I'll lose them out of mine."

I asked Rachel about acorns when we got back to the house. "Did Indians here eat acorns?"

"Yeah, a little bit. But, you know, you've got to rinse them and rinse them to get the tannins out. And even then, you know what?"

"What?"

"They taste like shit."

Then I was back on the plane, the puddle jumper, headed down to the university. I looked out the window as the snow disappeared and the landscape flattened out. I fumbled with something stiff in my coat pocket. I pulled it out, and it was a blue jay feather. A single feather like that, I thought, now that's loaded with ethnic connotations. God, I was starting to sound like Rachel. They'd held me captive, all of them, and had changed my once comfortable mentality into one of social and environmental conscience. It would take me weeks to get back to normal, I knew.

CHAPTER TWENTY-SEVEN
DEODORANT BEFORE COLUMBUS

"I got the package of jam you sent."

"Good."

"Thanks. The blackberry peach is my favorite."

"Should've sent two. I remember making it. It had been dry. Not enough blackberries to make a batch of jam, but I was surrounded by ripe peaches."

"I think of Zoey every time I eat it. I think it was her favorite."

"I think so, too."

"Have you heard from her?"

"No. Don't expect to."

"Where did they go?"

"Back to Chicago."

"I see. So, tell me about Manaboozhou's children."

"No."

"No?"

"No. We're not there yet."

"What do you mean?"

"I mean, you haven't even heard about his brothers and sisters yet."

"Is that required?"

"Yes. Each generation influences the generation that comes afterwards."

"But they're just stories."

"No they're not."

"OK."

"So Wiinona and the West Wind—they had these four sons."

"In four different generations."

"You're getting the hang of it.

"And the oldest son, he was kind of distant."

"What do you mean?"

"Well, he was the oldest one. And his parents practiced on him. They made all their mistakes on him. It influenced his personality a little bit, being the oldest one."

"Isn't this universal?"

"Of course it's universal. This story is probably thousands of years old. It probably wouldn't have survived if weren't universal."

"Are you making any of it up?"

"Only the details and the major points. Don't you trust me?"

"No."

"Well, it's tough being the oldest, you know. You've always got to change diapers and stuff. And your parents spend all of their money on the younger kids, who, by the way, get away with murder. Just ask Stella."

"No, I believe you."

"So, the oldest boy, his name was First Son, he eventually went off on his own, and the other brothers didn't see him very much. He helped his dad with the family business."

"Which was?"

"Wind."

"Oh yeah."

"Manaboozhou had a sister-in-law who was a real sweetheart."

"A sister-in-law?"

"I told you, he had parents, siblings, children, cousins, aunts, uncles. . . ."

"OK, OK."

"So the sister-in-law . . ."

"What was her name?"

"Jane Doe."

"Are you kidding?"

"She doesn't have a name here, not in this part of the story."

"Why not?"

"She doesn't need one here. Are you planning on mapping this whole thing out like a family tree, because you're going to be screwed if you even try it. I'll never sign off for the publisher."

"Why not?"

"Well, first of all, it's not linear like that. These people lived over thousands of years. They are still among us right now. They can't be mapped out like that.

"And, secondly, every wanna-be, every pseudo-Indian with a pencil would be trying to misuse the information to get a book out of it. I'm trusting you. I think you're a very intelligent human being. I'm depending upon you to do the right thing."

"Which is?"

"Never mind. I'll do the final edit."

"So, the sister-in-law . . ."

"She was married to Manaboozhou's older brother. He was the most beautiful boy she had ever seen, this one. He was the second-oldest son of Wiinona and Epanigiishimoog, and they called him Papageewiss, Middle Boy. His parents were really in love, and they knew they would have more children."

"And?"

"And she helped Manaboozhou get it together a little bit, when he was a young man. His grandmother was old as dirt, and she was happy to get him out of the house now and then."

"How did the sister-in-law help him?"

"Well, the first thing she did was teach him a little personal hygiene. I mean, he was sprouting hormones all over the place. He was too busy playing all the time to bathe. So she bugged him about it."

"And deodorant. She made him wear deodorant."

"Rachel, you're pulling my leg, aren't you?"

"What, you think Indians had B.O.?"

"Aw, c'mon, I've read the books. They had lice and, you know, all kinds of icky stuff. They lived in the woods with a lot of bugs."

"So how come the Indians had parasites, and the other guys didn't?"

"Hygiene."

"You think we didn't have hygiene? You think we didn't have soap? You think we didn't have deodorant? You think we didn't have shampoo? You think we didn't know how to deal with insects?

"Do you think that maybe, just maybe, your sources were describing displaced person camps? Do you think that maybe they were describing pitiful, clinging populations of tortured people crammed into little, bitty, crappy scraps of unwanted real estate? And before that, when de Soto's choniclers described towns on the Mississippi—at first they described thriving urban centers. Then, a couple of weeks later, they described tiny populations that had barely survived the measles epidemic they'd brought. People were sick and dying, and their biggest problem was coping with the huge piles of decomposing bodies that lay rotting all around them.

"This is what is wrong with history that only teaches the majority's side of things. You guys are left so ignorant. I hate educating you guys one at a time. . . ."

There it was again, "you guys." And there was that theme again, that she hated teaching us one at a time. I wasn't the bad guy. I was going out of my way to try to write a book about her people and their spirits. It was going to bring them respect. But she always had to bring in ugly things. I wanted others to see beauty in these people and their culture.

". . . So of course we had deodorant. The sister-in-law made stuff out of cedar roping."

"What kinds of things?"

"Bags, shirts, underwear, you name it."

"And?"

"And, this yellow powder falls off, when you make that roping. It's fine and aromatic and sweet. It's cedar powder, but without the prickly woody part. And it's waterproof. And you know how cedar repels insects and fights germs."

She was starting to make sense. "Rachel, where did you learn all this?"

"Well, the deodorant part came from a friend of mine. Her grandmother wouldn't use anything else, so her mother used to have to go out into the woods and get it, after the old lady couldn't do it herself."

"You mean, the deodorant part isn't really part of the story?"

"Of course it's part of the story. *That* grandmother, her great-great-grandmother was Manaboozhou's sister-in-law. Stop acting like you know more about this stuff than I do."

"I'm sorry."

CHAPTER TWENTY-EIGHT
BOYS WILL BE BOYS

"He died."

    "Who?"

    "Papageewiss."

"How?"

"He was out messing around with his brothers."

"And?"

"Great boyfriend, fun guy to date. Not much of a husband. Didn't work much. Always played."

"And?"

"Music."

"Music?"

"Music. He was addicted to it. Spent all his time concocting melodies. We still sing them today. He taught us about the music in the trees, the music of the soft winds. He taught us about rhythm—the rhythm of waves close by, little ones, lapping, and waves far off, big ones pounding the shore and making the earth shake. Rhythms . . ."

And Rachel began to sing, softly at first. They were nonsense syllables. "Gotta teach you the tune, first," she'd say. She picked up a flat drum and blew the dust off it. She produced a wide variety of sounds with the small drum.

"Made by Fat Boy, the best Ojibwe drummaker in the Midwest."

"You rank them?"

"No. I'm just being nice. How'd you like to be known for hundreds of miles around as 'Fat Boy'?"

"Seems kind of cruel."

"Yeah, but he likes it."

"Was Papageewiss fat?"

"Oh, just a wee bit overweight. He didn't get as much exercise as the other boys, because he was always playing around making music. We value him for that, you know. Being a good provider was not his strong point. Music was his strong point. We have to at least give that to him, not judge him by our own standards of whether or not he could hunt."

"Did he hunt?"

"In a pinch. But I told you, music was his strong point. And clothes. He was a flashy dresser."

"He was a flashy dresser?"

"Yeah. Before he was married, girls were always bringing him presents—leggings with moosehair embroidery, things like that. He loved to wear clothes with flowers and shiny things on them, kind of like Elvis. He was a really great musician."

"Elvis?"

"Papageewiss."

"OK."

"So, one day First Son was home visiting. It was late spring, and Epanigiishimoog was due for some doldrums. So First Son, he came home to Grandmother's lodge, and he made the rounds visiting his brothers."

"And?"

"And they got to showing off, because that's what brothers do. Papageewiss's wife and Grandmother were at Grandmother's house boiling up some grouse eggs, and they were cooking wild rice with garlic. It was just a little snack for lunch.

"And the more athletic of the two boys started teasing him. They talked him into going out onto thin ice. They were on the south side of a lake, where the shore was protected from the sun by some trees and bushes. The sun was still pretty far south. So the ice came right up almost to shore. And those boys, they just hopped right over that water at the edge onto the ice sheet.

"It's really kind of neat when it's thin like that. It's shoved up into a rolling surface by the water from below, so there are high peaks with nothing but air underneath them. If you're really fast, you can skitter right across them, and back into the valleys again, where the water supports your weight on the ice. It's a really neat thing to do, but you've really got to know the lake well. Actually, it's a pretty stupid thing to do, but those boys, they did it. You know, we all do things that we don't tell our mothers about. No sense worrying them, after something didn't go wrong."

"I see."

"So, the two athletic brothers, they knew the lake really well. They'd fished it dozens of times. They knew every shallow, every dropoff . . . and they thought it would be really funny to send Papageewiss where he'd fall in over his head.

"They had a rope. But he was out too far, and they'd stayed out too long. The sun was breaking up the ice all around them. They could hear it under the surface of the lake, like the roaring of a waterfall almost. And they laid down on their stomachs, and they reached out the rope to him. But the water was cold, and maybe he wasn't in as good physical shape as his brothers, and they lost him. When they came back to the house, they were crying."

"That's horrible."

"Yeah. And then he showed up at the house."

"Who?"

"Papageewiss."

"As a ghost?"

"No, as a fish."

"What?"

"He could change himself into anything else that he wanted to, so he changed himself into a big pike. He was kind of vain, you know, because he'd gotten all those presents from girls over the years. So he didn't just change himself into a pike, he changed himself into a really big pike."

"And?"

"And he shook fish slime all over the house."

"You're kidding, right?"

"No. Manaboozhou was standing right there, with his mouth hanging open. And a bunch of pike slime went right into his mouth. Pike are slimy on purpose, so they can hide in the weeds and wait for their prey."

"And?"

"And Manaboozhou was spitting out fish slime, which really isn't that bad when it's fresh, and he was saying, 'Papageewiss, you've pushed it too far this time. I'm going to get you, and when I get you, it's going to be bammity, bammity, bammity, bammity.' So Papageewiss took off."

"And?"

"I'm not telling."

"What do you mean you're not telling?"

"You can't have it."

"Why not?"

"It's not your story. It's our story."

"Did he catch him?"

"Maybe."

"Maybe?"

"Maybe not."

"But he lived?"

"Maybe—for a while . . ."

"Rachel, you're not being fair!"

"And they killed the next brother, too."

"What?"

"In horseplay. Chibiaboozhou, the Dead Son, they drowned him."

"Thin ice?"

"Uh huh."

"How?"

"A race. They challenged him to a race across the lake. They just coerced him into going too far. They stopped, turned, and ran back toward shore. But he was delighted, because he'd never gotten out front and beaten them before. So he didn't look back, because he didn't want to lose his momentum. That was their plan, you see, they let him get ahead, so that it would happen."

"They *tried* to drown him?"

"No, they just wanted to dunk him."

"What horrible brothers."

"Yeah, but we love 'em."

"But, they didn't learn by their mistakes."

"No, but I guess we could."

CHAPTER TWENTY-NINE

HOLES-IN-THE-SKY

Sometimes I miss them. I miss their noise, their rudeness, and the excess prosody in their speech. I remember one time when I had begged Rachel to tell me a story, so she told me about holes in the sky. The sun had broken through the clouds after one long, overcast day. She pointed to the break in the cloud cover. "There's one, a hole in the sky."

"That's beautiful."

"But the word for sky is a homonym for the word for day. And there was this guy named Hole-in-the-Sky, and, and . . ." She giggled.

"And?"

"And some idiot translated it into Hole-in-the-Day."

"Isn't he like a famous chief or something?"

"A famous *what?*"

"Sorry."

"Forgiven."

"Actually, I think Hole-in-the-Day sounds sort of romantic."

"Unforgiven!" Stella jumped in. "I think it sounds simplistic. Like 'Ugh, heap big chief, and me go look for bear over hill.'"

"I never thought of it that way, Stella." Guilt. She brought it on, just like her mother.

Rachel broke the tension. "Well, it's a good thing it wasn't a homophone for 'head'!"

Stella burst out laughing, "Hole-in-the-Head!"

"*Chief* Hole-in-the-Head!" Rachel wheezed.

"How about bucket?" Isabel threw herself on the bed.

And there they were, laughing hysterically, tangled up in a heap of squirming bodies, singing, "There's a hole in my he-ead, Dear Liza, Dear Liza. . . ."

"How about butt?" Rachel gasped out, and they threw themselves into another frenzy.

"There's a hole in my he-ead, Chief Butt-Head, Chief Butt-Head. . . ."

Little Jack jumped up and down on the mattress, singing, "Butt hole, butt hole . . ."

"Good thing the guy never shot himself in the foot," Stella moaned, and they went on again.

Little Jack continued to bounce and sing, "Butt hole, butt hole . . ."

The list went on and on.

"Muffler!"

"Sock!"

"Boat!"

"Hot Air Balloon!"

"Nostril!"

"Gosh," said Rachel, "I hope he didn't have any male children."

"I don't get it," said Zoey.

"Like toe truck, Z. Like a big truck shaped like a toe."

"I get that part. I don't understand why he wouldn't want to have any male children."

Isabel draped herself over her slim companion. "Because, Z, nobody wants to have a stupid name like 'Me go look for bear over hill.'"

"I get it."

And she did.

CHAPTER THIRTY
MATH AND SNAKES

Trying to phone Rachel is almost always futile. It either rings and rings, or it's busy. I used to try leaving messages with the children, but Rachel informed me that it is a foolish thing to do. Even when I get through, she doesn't always come to the phone. Stella once informed me that her parents were butchering a deer, and that the thermometer next to the barn had read almost fifty degrees at dawn, so they weren't talking to anybody. Sometimes Stella would lie for her mother. She wasn't a very good liar. "Uh, she's not here," she would say, followed by a long silence. Stella was the gracious one: she usually sang out, "Oh, HI! How are you?" when she heard my voice. She could make small talk. Isabel wouldn't.

"Hello?"

"Hello. Rachel?"

"No."

"Stella?"

"No."

"Z?"

"Do you wanna try the dog next?"

"Sorry, Izzy."

"I know, we all sound alike."

"Is your mother at home?"

"No."

"When do you think she'll be back?"

"Don't know."

"Is she out of town?"

"No."

"In Traverse City?"

"No."

"Come on, Izzy, help me out here. I'm trying to figure out when to call back."

"She went to the post office to mail a box of apples to Stella."

I could imagine that it was a big box, probably a copier paper box. I could visualize Rachel lining the box with bubble wrap. She used to collect it from merchants she knew, and store it in a huge bushel basket next to a shelf full of canning jars in the far end of the living room. She used it for mailing her baskets. Periodically, her children would pull out long sheets of the wrap, line them up on the wooden floors of the long room, then run back and forth over the bubbles, popping them with their bare feet. Lala would jump and bark. I imagined Stella would do the same thing with her friends at college, after she ate the apples.

"So, how have you been, Izzy?"

"OK."

"Do you know any good Indian stories?"

"No. I'm not a good Indian."

"So, what are you doing in school?"

"N formulas."

"Are they hard?"

"No. My mom uses them in her basket work all the time. She has to prime factorize the number of stitches in the rim to determine the spacing on the handles and the loops. It doesn't always work out even, so sometimes she has to do an N formula."

"I see."

"You know, like Gauss."

"I see."

"Didn't she ever tell you the Gauss formula?"

"Is it a traditional story?"

"Yup."

"The snake story?"

"Yup."

"How does it end?"

"Where did you leave off?"

"I don't know."

"Do you want to talk to my mom?"

"Is she there?"

"Here."

"Hi."

"Rachel?"

"Hi."

"So, you mailed apples to Stella?"

"Yeah. They cost a dollar apiece in the vending machine at school."

"Where is she?"

"MIT."

"MIT? How is she handling the big city?"

"Doesn't go out much. I told her to try to imagine the sound of cars going by as the sound of waves. It's what I did in college."

"I see. Was it a big box of apples?"

"I send a half bushel every week. She leaves the box outside her door, and her neighbors help themselves. Good crop this year. No sense them going to waste. Some of the apple varieties are biennial. We have eight different kinds, you know."

"Isabel likes math."

"No. She could care less. She does it well, though."

Rachel had insisted that Ojibwe was the language of math nerds. She claimed that the Ojibwe had names for all sorts of curves and mathematical sequences.

"Sine generated curve."

"What?"

"Sine generated curve."

"What about it?"

"One time Manaboozhou got a hole in his birch bark canoe. Happens all the time. They require a lot of maintenance if you use them a lot.

"He was aping around with a mink. The mink was on this old dead log at the edge of the water, running back and forth along it, to get a good look at Manaboozhou."

"I see."

"So the mink called out, 'Nice canoe, bring it over closer here, so I can see it.' And being the vain fool that he was, Manaboozhou paddled right on over there.

"Mink sat right up on his hind legs and looked into the canoe. So Manaboozhou sat right up in a squat like that and looked back at Mink. Then Mink danced on the log. So Manaboozhou danced in the bottom of his canoe. Then Mink hopped up and down on one foot. Then Manaboozhou hopped up and down on one foot.

"It was too much weight in one place. It split the interior cedar sheathing, and his foot went through the bottom of the canoe.

"Then the mink changed itself back into Papageewiss, and he laughed until he was in pain.

"His canoe was around the next bend in the shoreline, and he towed his brother's canoe home. So Manaboozhou sat in Papageewiss's canoe and held the tow rope."

"And?"

"And, if you do it right, it tows in a sine generated curve. Diidii . . . diidii . . .'"

"Deedee?"

We were driving to town at the time, and Rachel moved the steering wheel back and forth slightly, quickly repeating, "diidiidiidiidiidii . . . ," causing the small car to move correspondingly. Fortunately, Rachel rarely drives over thirty-five miles per hour. She doesn't like traveling faster than she can move herself under her own power.

"This gave Manaboozhou an idea, so he said, 'Papageewiss, pull the canoe into that sandy stretch of shore right there.' Then he changed himself into a snake the color of red dirt and slithered under a rock.

"Papageewiss was even more vain than his brother. He was very, very insecure. Whenever he let somebody else sing one of his songs, he always made them say in a big voice first, that the song belonged to him, Papageewiss. If people didn't, he could get pretty mean about it.

"So, anyhow, he couldn't be outdone by his *little* brother, so he changed himself into a snake the color of red dirt with black stripes.

"But Manaboozhou knew he was stronger than his big brother, and he didn't want to let him forget it. So he changed himself into a snake the color of red dirt with black stripes and white stripes. It was a really good color scheme, and a lot of snakes still use it to this day."

"And?"

"It's a lot like Gauss, I think."

"Gauss?"

"N times N-plus-one over two."

"What?"

"One, plus two, plus three, plus four . . ."

"OK."

"When I was in graduate school, I used to sit up in the tower in the library and read Gauss. It was in German. It wasn't translated."

"What does this have to do with this story?"

"I was reading all these letters back and forth, between him and a friend of his from Czechoslovakia, who was also a mathematician. They really had a lot of fun. They just kept feeding off of one another's ideas and kept going back and forth, like two boys trying to see who could pee uphill the farthest."

"Did Manaboozhou and his brother do this?"

"I'm sure they did. But this day, they were changing into snakes first. And Papageewiss was so self-absorbed that he changed himself into a really, really big snake. He was so big, that it was impractical. That was one of his faults—he could only think in terms of scale. He always thought that bigger was better, and he never knew when to quit."

"And?"

"And—you'd better wash the windows, while I pump the gas."

"*Then*, will you finish the story?"

"See that school down the road there? One time, I was substituting there, and the principal mistook me for an Indian parent that she'd had a fight with. And she grabbed me by the shirt and started pulling me out of the room in front of all the students. She had a reputation for being that way. It was like being an administrator wasn't big enough for her; she had to be the boss of all the people who she thought were weaker than her. Maybe this other Indian mother was pretty competitive, too, so the principal thought she had to smash her and destroy her.

"After she finally figured out I wasn't the same woman, she was still mean, you know, to cover up her mistakes. She made horrible threats to me. She said I scared people because I was an Indian. She said I had to notify her secretary in writing every time I left the classroom, even if it was to go to the bathroom. Do you think she told the white substitute teachers to do that?"

"Probably not. What did you do?"

"I turned into a snake the color of red dirt and hid under a rock."

"What about the rest of the story?"

"Papageewiss kept changing himself back and forth into different animals, but it never worked out. Eventually he changed himself back into the big snake, because he saw a rock that was big enough to hide himself under."

"And?"

"And Manaboozhou told the Thunderbirds to send down several thunderbolts to smash the big rock into a bunch of little rocks."

"And?"

"And, it got out of hand. Papageewiss was smashed and killed."

CHAPTER THIRTY-ONE
THE WIINDIGOOG

"Rachel, you could be of more help to me, if you didn't hate education so much."

"I don't hate education. I love education. I love the social aspect of it. I love its history. I love its law. I love changing it. I love teaching. I love teaching my babies. . . ."

She was off on a long one.

"Did I ever tell you about Blue Duck?"

"No."

"Blue Duck is a town. It's a real town. But it didn't used to be."

"What does that mean?"

"The Indians, they didn't want to send their kids on the train."

"What?"

"To school. They didn't want to send their kids on the train to school. It's a horrible beast, a train . . . big, and metal, and loud. Can you imagine climbing on and off of one as a kid? Can you imagine doing it in the dark, when the winter days are short?"

"No."

"But they did, those kids. They had to. Off they went to the boarding school. It was mandatory. It wasn't that long ago. I was alive then. Those train wheels, they could cut you in two, if you messed up. And they only gave you a couple of minutes to climb on.

"The train only went by once a day, in one direction. So you went on the train, and you stayed at the school all week. It was awful. Could you imagine not being with your mom and dad all the time like that? If you

141

had kids, you'd know what it's like to be away from them, to worry about them every minute. It's not a very nice thing to do to families. They were going to civilize us. Not a very civilized method, was it?"

More and more information was coming out about Indian boarding schools. They were not necessarily nice places.

"Was it nice, or was it like the stories that are coming out?"

"It was OK, I guess. I don't want to talk about that."

"Did you or other kids in your family have problems there?"

"I don't want to talk about that right now. The fact is, that it was a really crummy thing to do to families—*any* families. I mean, we're even figuring out that it's not a very good thing to do to primates in general. Don't you agree?"

"I guess I would."

"So, they took all of the kids from all of the towns on the train line, and they sent them to a central school. But then, these terrible Wiindigoog came."

"What are they?"

"Beasts. Horrible, starving beasts."

"What do they look like?"

"Sometimes they look like people, but with really big, sharp teeth and very messy hair. And they wear these really long, dark robes, with funny hats and white collars. . . ."

"Are you describing nuns and priests?"

"Never."

"Rachel, you're lying to me!"

"OK, OK, so they didn't wear black robes. But you've got to admit, it would make them scarier."

"And?"

"And this one Indian, he got this really stupid idea to challenge them to a race."

"Across the lake?"

"Yup."

"Did it work?"

"No."

"No?"

"No. The guy lost the race."

"Did he drown?"

"Does it matter?"

"Does it?"

"No, because the race was really about wagering. The man had bet that if he won the race, the Wiindigoog would go away. And they said, 'Well, if you lose, we get to eat everybody.' And he lost. So, the Wiindigoog ate all the grownups first, because they were the slowest, and they were the juiciest and the tastiest.

"And there was this whole town, with nothing but children running around and screaming, 'No! Don't eat me!' The only grownup left alive was this old granny, because she was so skinny. So she would feed the children to give them strength to keep running. And if the children held on to the granny, they were at safety, and the Wiindigoog couldn't eat them. But they always slowed the grandmother down, so she pushed them away. And then the children weren't safe any more. And the Wiindigoog were always bigger than the children, like fifth or sixth grade maybe, so they could outrun them. Only those Wiindigoog couldn't eat all those children all at once, so they froze them for later, just like a big ol' rump roast. And when the grandmother fed the frozen kids, they started running all over the place again, so those Wiindigoog hardly ever won."

"So, there was this town where everybody played freeze tag?"

"Yeah. But then the parents decided they didn't want their kids to go away on the train any more, so they quit sending them. All of them. They all quit, just like that."

"Smart move."

"No. The train quit stopping at those towns, and nobody got any supplies any more. No mail, no medical goods, nothing."

"That's horrible."

"I was away at college."

"Really?"

"Yeah, so they told everybody that they had to move. They'd set up a reserve for them over at Blue Duck. And all these people from miles around crowded into this little reserve at Blue Duck, because it was right near the school."

"So the families got to keep their children at home with them at night. It sounds like a pretty good thing to me."

"Yeah, it was great." She was deadpan.

"What do you mean?"

"Well, they weren't back in their old homes. You can't move everything. You can't move the lakes and the dropoffs where the fish hang out. And you can't move the game trails. You can't move an old sawbuck that's just hanging on by a thread, but would've worked for a few more years anyhow. You can't move the graves. The graves are supposed to be fed regularly. You can't move your roots, and you can't move the stories. Every rock outcropping, every big tree, every inch of shore, it's got a story—about human interaction and love and hate and successes and mistakes. . . .

"There were people already there, too, you know. Can you imagine how hard it was for them to have all those other Indians all on top of them like that? On top of their favorite fishing and hunting spots, their berry bushes, their stories, their memories?

"It's been a generation and a half now. A lot of those people from Blue Duck, they're all messed up. People from Blue Duck have a reputation for not getting along with one another, for fighting all the time, for alcoholism. They're wandering around, poor souls, like those tired children with the Wiindigoog chasing them."

"These stories are gruesome."

"I told you, they're preventive. The gruesome ones are preventive. You're the one who wanted these traditional stories. I told you, they still exist, because they reflect the present. I'm not pulling any punches. You just didn't know what you were getting into."

"So, can't the people at Blue Duck do something about their problems?"

"They try. But they don't have the same resources that they had a generation and a half ago. They were compressed into a smaller package of resources. You're expecting them to do more with less. That's very racist of you. I know you don't mean to be, but it's racist, in a subtle way."

"I didn't do it Rachel. I was just a kid. It was the generation before me."

"Well, then, I guess we can learn by *their* mistakes."

MANABOOZHOU'S CHILDREN

"Tell me about Manaboozhou's wife."

"Nothing much to tell. She was normal."

"She was married to someone who was half spirit."

"We've been through this. Spirit is just an English substitute for the real meaning of the word."

"OK, she was married to a man who was half mystery."

"Sounds pretty normal to me."

"Rachel, give me a break."

"What do you want to hear? Do you want to hear that she was special?"

"Yes."

"OK, she was special."

"But, she *was*."

"And why would that be?"

"Because of the things that were always happening around her. She was married to a son of the wind. Strange things happened all the time. You said so yourself. You said that Manaboozhou was always messing up."

"Well, I guess you'd have to be pretty strong to put up with all of those mishaps, wouldn't you?"

"Exceptional."

"People probably don't give her half the credit she deserves, you know."

"Or the kids, either. The kids must have been great."

"Yeah, they were all math nerds. So were all of the generations that came after them."

"You can't make that kind of generalization."

CHAPTER THIRTY-TWO

"OK, they all lived on welfare, and they all went to college for free."

"You guys go to college for free?"

"Welfare myth."

"Tell me about Manaboozhou's children."

"Normal."

"Normal?"

"Normal. They were a lot like my kids."

"And?"

"Do you want to hear about the seven generations of the Ojibwe?"

"Absolutely."

"Wiinona and Epanigiishimoog had four sons, each one born in a different generation."

"I know."

"Be quiet, or I won't tell you."

"OK."

"The fifth generation is made up of the people we have seen pass away in our lifetimes. We are the sixth generation. The ones we have seen born in our lifetimes are the seventh generation.

"We have all kinds of celebrations for our babies, for the seventh generation. Boy, it's great being a little kid in an Ojibwe family, because everybody does everything for me, me, me. Keep the environment clean, for *me*. Be a respectful person and a good parent, for *me*. Learn the old stories and keep the traditions, for *me*.

"Then, at about age twelve or so, responsibilities start piling on. And somebody tells you the truth."

"Which is what?"

"We are only the sixth generation. We have responsibilities to those who come after us."

ABOUT THE AUTHOR

Lois Beardslee has been a teacher and writer for twenty-five years. She is also an accomplished artist whose works are in public and private collections worldwide. She is the author of *Lies to Live By*.